General editor: Graham Handley MA Ph.D.

Brodie's Notes on Alan Sillitoe's

Selected Fiction

Saturday Night and Sunday Morning, The Loneliness of the Long-Distance Runner, and A Sillitoe Selection

Andrew Copping BA, MA(Oxon.)
Head of English at Woodhouse Grove School, Bradford

G000141851

Pan Books London, Sydney and Auckland

Acknowledgements My thanks to Grafton Books and the author, Alan Sillitoe, for permission to reproduce extracts from *Saturday Night and Sunday Morning* and *The Loneliness of the Long-Distance Runner*. The author would like to thank Dr Graham Handley for his generous contribution to this Note.

First published 1991 by
Pan Books Ltd, Cavaye Place, London sw10 9pg

9 8 7 6 5 4 3 2 1

© Pan Books Ltd 1991

ISBN 0 330 50326 x

Photoset by Parker Typesetting Service, Leicester

Printed in England by Clays Ltd, St Ives plc

This book is sold subject to the condition that it shall not,
by way of trade or otherwise, be lent, re-sold, hired out
or otherwise circulated without the publisher's prior consent
in any form of binding or cover other than that in which
it is published and without a similar condition including this
condition being imposed on the subsequent purchaser

Contents

£2.50

References in these Notes are to the Grafton
edition of the books, but references
are also given to particular parts and chapters, so that
the Notes may be used with any edition of the novel.

Preface by the general editor

The intention throughout this study aid is to stimulate and guide, to encourage your involvement in the book, and to develop informed responses and a sure understanding of the main details.

Brodie's Notes provide a clear outline of the play or novel's plot, followed by act, scene, or chapter summaries and/or commentaries. These are designed to emphasize the most important literary and factual details. Poems, stories or non-fiction texts combine brief summary with critical commentary on individual aspects or common features of the genre being examined. Textual notes define what is difficult or obscure and emphasize literary qualities. Revision questions are set at appropriate points to test your ability to appreciate the prescribed book and to write accurately and relevantly about it.

In addition, each of these Notes includes a critical appreciation of the author's art. This covers such major elements as characterization, style, structure, setting and themes. Poems are examined technically – rhyme, rhythm, for instance. In fact, any important aspect of the prescribed work will be evaluated. The aim is to send you back to the text you are studying.

Each study aid concludes with a series of general questions which require a detailed knowledge of the book: some of these questions may invite comparison with other books, some will be suitable for coursework exercises, and some could be adapted to work you are doing on another book or books. Each study aid has been adapted to meet the needs of the current examination requirements. They provide a basic, individual and imaginative response to the work being studied, and it is hoped that they will stimulate you to acquire disciplined reading habits and critical fluency.

Graham Handley 1991

Literary terms used in these Notes

adopting a persona When a writer writes as if he is a character in the story. This is seen throughout *Loneliness* and, at times, in *Saturday*.

cliché A trite or over-used expression which has become lifeless as a result.

colloquialism A word, phrase or expression used in everyday speech. The colloquial style is plain and relaxed.

imagery Comparisons between two or more usually unrelated ideas in order to create mental images for, and extend the understanding of, the reader.

metaphor A way of describing something in which one thing is said to *be* the other thing with which it is compared. One example in *Saturday* is when Arthur describes Brenda's being pregnant as her having 'a bun in the oven' (Chapter 5). (This is also a colloquialism!)

narrative technique The way in which the story is told – i.e. use of colloquialism, cliché, imagery, etc (see above).

naturalism and realism Terms used to describe literature which attempts to portray life as it really is.

simile A means of description where a point (or points) of likeness between two different things is brought out. An example is when Mrs Bull's persistent knocking at the door is described as being 'like a machine-gun' (Chapter 8).

symbolism When an object or incident might be seen as representing something else. A notable example is the cross-country running in *Loneliness* which also represents the difficult, arduous and isolated nature of Smith's life.

The author and his work

Alan Sillitoe was born in Nottingham in 1928, 'in the front bedroom of a red-bricked council house'. His father was an illiterate tanner and Sillitoe was one of five children. He did not shine at school, though he did once win fourpence for an English essay on a warehouse fire. He left school at fourteen to work in the Raleigh Bicycle Factory; after working in various factories, he was appointed, at seventeen, as an air traffic control assistant with the Ministry of Aircraft Production at Langar Airfield. He enlisted in May 1946 in the Royal Air Force Volunteer Reserve, and spent eighteen months on active service in Malaya as a wireless operator, during which time the communist guerrillas began an insurrection against the British occupying forces. At the end of 1949 he was invalided out of the service with tuberculosis.

It was in the RAF hospital at Wroughton that he began a 'feverish bout of urgent writing'. By twenty-two, he had completed a four-hundred-page novel, *By What Road*, which was 'chaotic' and rejected by publishers without comment. In 1950 he met a nineteen-year-old American girl, who was also a writer and poet, named Ruth Fainlight (whom he later married). Using his Air Force pension, they decided to live near the south coast of France. In 1952 they left England for France and one year later went to Majorca. There Sillitoe met the successful writer Robert Graves (best known for his novel *I, Claudius*) who asked him: 'Why don't you write a book set in Nottingham, which is something you know about?' After seven unpublished novels Sillitoe heeded this advice and in the summer of 1956 he wrote his final version of *Saturday Night and Sunday Morning*. Five publishers rejected it, but in 1958, almost ten years after he had begun writing seriously, it finally appeared – and was voted the best first novel of the year. *The Loneliness of the Long-Distance Runner*, which won the Hawthornden Prize for Literature, came out the following year. Both were popular and both were made into films.

With his wife, Alan Sillitoe now divides his time between London and a house in Kent, and since 1959 he has produced many further works (over thirty publications) of prose, poetry and drama. Most of his work is, as *The Times* wrote of *Loneliness*, 'graphic, tough, outspoken, informal' and a good deal of his work involves characters from grim lacklustre Nottingham whose environment often consists of a dull drab monotony. His novels mirror the atmosphere he grew up in or his later experiences and are uncompromising, uneasy and even disturbing. They have been much praised by critics as being 'very much the real thing' (*New Statesman*) and he is possibly the first writer to deal with the 1950s working man seriously and convincingly and not just as a caricature. The accurate portrayal of life gives all his novels and short stories a sense of truth, even if it is often painful truth.

[Unacknowledged quotations by Sillitoe are taken from his autobiographical essay *The Long Piece*.]

The fifties: A decade of increasingly angry young men

Though of immense contemporary relevance, both *Saturday Night* and *Loneliness* are very much a product of, and reaction to, the decade in which they were written. Before examining them, it is helpful and revealing to look at the events, circumstances and beliefs of that decade. The nineteen-fifties was a decade in which the keyword was change. Even so, by the end of the decade life was still very different from today. The average weekly wage in 1959 was £11 2s 6d (approximately £11.13) – so Arthur Seaton's £14 a week was 'comfortable' indeed – and a First Division professional footballer was restricted to a maximum weekly wage of £20. The Common Market was not formed until 1958 and it was not until the same year that stereophonic recording (as it was then called) was pioneered. For most of the decade more people listened to the wireless (words such as 'transistor' and 'radio' were little known) than watched television. Calculators and computers were at a very embryonic stage and few would have heard of them, never mind owned or known how to use them. The first stretch, from London to Birmingham, of the country's first motorway, the M1, was not opened until 1959. The first creature, the Eskimo dog Laika, to orbit the earth did so in November 1957 and, in 1958, *Explorer*, America's first earth satellite, was launched; the world had to wait until 1961 before Major Yuri Gagarin made the first human flight into space.

Philosophically, the decade witnessed an increased uncertainty: for many, hope was replaced by scepticism. Previously held beliefs, such as patriotism and the inevitable victory of just causes, seemed increasingly untenable. The main reason for this was the ever-present dread of the nuclear threat. In the mushroom clouds of Nagasaki and Hiroshima the hopes of the first half of the century dissolved. America and Russia embarked on the Cold War (a state of political tension and rivalry stopping short of actual full-scale war), the nuclear arms race began in earnest, and to many a cataclysmic World War Three did not seem far away. People had good reason to worry. In January 1956, the US Secretary of State, John Foster Dulles, declared: 'The ability to get to the verge without getting into the war is the

3

necessary art. If you are scared to go to the brink you are lost.'
Russia took the world to the brink later in 1956 when it invaded
Hungary, and Britain's, albeit brief, sending of troops to attack
Egypt during the Suez crisis did not alleviate the sense of
danger. Neither did Nevil Shute's frightening 1957 novel, *On the
Beach*, in which he foresaw the extermination of the human race
owing to nuclear war. It was not a fanciful idea: by 1960,
America and Russia between them had enough nuclear missiles
and bombs to bring about the state known as Mutually Assured
Destruction (or MAD for short).

Not surprisingly, many felt confused and the youth of the
fifties were forced to re-assess their aims in life. Consequently,
convention was more frequently challenged and, for many of
the younger generation, personal pleasure began to be seen as
more important than national pride; this later tendency can be
seen in both Arthur Seaton and Smith. The increased rebelliousness of the young is evident in the crime figures for offen-
ders under 21 in England: in 1955 they totalled 24,000; by 1959
they had nearly doubled to 45,000.

As so often in history, culture reflected the times, and one can
find many examples of the increased rebelliousness and importance of the young. As early as 1951, in America, the story of a
sixteen-year-old rebel, Holden Caulfield, expelled from three
schools and intent on enjoying New York's night-life, appeared
in J. D. Salinger's *The Catcher in the Rye*. Films brought Marlon
Brando in *The Wild One* (1954), as a precursor of Hell's Angels
(violent and lawless motorcycle gangs), and also that lasting
image of fifties' rebellion, James Dean. He appeared in only four
films, including the appropriately titled *Rebel Without a Cause*
(1955), before dying in a car crash at the age of twenty-four, and
yet he captured the spirit of the age; the American writer, John
Dos Passos, described him well: 'the resentful hair ... the deep
eyes floating in lonesomeness, the bitter beat look, the scorn on
the lip.'

In 1955, the film *Blackboard Jungle* appeared in Britain, containing Bill Haley's 'Rock Around the Clock'. The song sounds
tame now, but then Rock and Roll was a new phenomenon, and
the song caused a furore, being adopted as the anthem of
dissident youth (for whom the newly coined word 'teenager'
became increasingly used). In it they saw a rejection of the old
values and of the values of the old. Elvis Presley became the

'King' of Rock and Roll and, in the sixties, President J. F. Kennedy described him as being, in the fifties, 'a symbol of vitality [and] rebelliousness' of America. He was only allowed to appear on television from the waist upwards as his sexually provocative pelvic movements were deemed to be a dangerous threat to public morals. None the less, despite his rebelliousness, he willingly – unlike Arthur Seaton and his cousins – did his military service (compulsory for all men, unless disabled, in both America and Britain in the fifties) in 1958.

Cultural rebellion and change occurred elsewhere. The word 'pop' was coined and Pop Art (painted by such as Richard Hamilton and Peter Blake) appeared. In America, the Beat Generation arrived and the works of Kerouac (notably, *On the Road*, 1957), Ginsberg and Burroughs rejected wage-earning and conventionality, and sought freedom in nomadic hitch-hiking, sexual permissiveness and general immorality.

More importantly as regards Sillitoe, in Britain literature saw the advent of Angry Young Men. Their works involved various forms of social alienation and, according to the novelist Doris Lessing, provided 'an injection of vitality into the withered arm of British literature'. Writers such as John Osborne in the play *Look Back in Anger* (first performed in 1956), Kingsley Amis in *Lucky Jim* (1954), Colin Wilson in *The Outsider* (1956) and John Braine in *Room at the Top* (1957) reacted against the cosy middle-class world of so much literature of the time and shook the nation with their radical and anarchic views, their emphasis on domestic realism and their presentation of the lower middle class and the class war. Their works were popular and the portrayal of the 'hero' (or anti-hero as he was sometimes called) as a protesting malcontent or as an immoral opportunist stirred the thoughts of a nation. Sillitoe himself has often been described as an Angry Young Man and, though he himself disagrees with the label, undoubtedly both *Saturday Night* and *Loneliness* took the presentation of the working man, the Outlaw, the self-concerned pleasure-seeker, further than ever before.

As well as a cultural revolution, the fifties witnessed a social revolution. At the beginning of the decade there was severe food rationing, even worse than it had been in 1945, and there were many shortages of such necessities as houses and coal. With the Chancellor, Sir Stafford Cripps, demanding further sacrifices, life was bleaker than it had been in wartime. And yet by the end of the decade Britain had recovered from the ravages of wartime to such an extent that this age of austerity was replaced by one of unprecedented affluence. By 1957, the Prime Minister, Harold Macmillan, was able to tell the country: 'You've never had it so good.' Luxury goods were now readily available to many: in 1950, only 350,000 households had televisions – by 1959, 60 per cent; in 1958, hire-purchase restrictions were abolished and a person could own a car for a down-payment of as little as £4 8s. 5d (approximately £4.42); and Arthur Seaton was easily able to indulge his taste for expensive clothes.

Overall, maybe the fifties is most notable for being a decade when people, especially the young, began to question the establishment and the accepted *status quo*, and began to look out for themselves. Women, long consigned to the kitchen, began to realize they were getting a poor deal. Marriage was still seen by many, like Doreen in *Saturday Night*, as the main aim in life, but not all were prepared to seek complete satisfaction in marriage any more and many looked for greater social and economic equality. Brenda's seeking adulterous satisfaction is a very limited and minor example of the sexual revolution, but the fact of her readily looking outside her marriage for excitement and adventure was something which would have been much more unlikely at the start of the decade. This questioning of the establishment and previously accepted values was seen elsewhere: in 1958 the Campaign for Nuclear Disarmament was launched; and even royalty, revered as above criticism by the vast majority until then, was savagely attacked by that Angry Young Man, John Osborne: 'My objection to the royalty symbol is that it is dead: it is the gold filling in a mouthful of decay.' All of this questioning and change helps to explain the creation of fictional characters such as Arthur Seaton and Smith. Though very different from one another, they shared common traits: like many of their generation, they felt antagonistic to authority; like many of their class, they became aware of the unfairness of their circumstances; and, like many, they became selfish and sought only self-indulgent and short-lived pleasures. Perhaps the philosophy underlying the late fifties, the time of *Saturday Night* and *Loneliness*, is best summed up by the title of a famous, popular and highly acclaimed 1959 film, *I'm All Right, Jack*. Certainly, the publication of *Saturday Night* and *Loneliness* provided more shocking, unavoidable and undeniable truths about a certain stratum of society than had occurred before in literature. Consequently, they are both the products of the changes of the fifties and indicators of further change.

The films

Both films are worthy of note and they do help to throw further light on the texts. They are especially useful in terms of re-creating the atmosphere of the time. We are able to witness the living conditions, the clothes, the hairstyles and Nottingham itself: they provide a helpfully accurate visual representation of the texts. As films, though, they are works of art in their own right (it is important to remember this when watching them) and both differ from the texts from which they were originally taken – presumably with Alan Sillitoe's blessing, however, as he wrote the screenplays for both.

The more successful film is *Saturday Night and Sunday Morning* (1960) directed by Karel Reisz and starring Albert Finney as Arthur, Shirley Anne Field as Doreen and Rachel Roberts as Brenda. It created a stir on release – partly because of the rebelliousness of Arthur and partly because it displayed a new attitude to sex – and, indeed, *Halliwell's Film Guide* declares: 'It transformed British cinema and was much imitated.' It sim-plifies and compresses the novel, changes the sequence of events (it starts in the factory and then moves to the drinking match, for example, and Doreen appears in the first ten minutes), and omits certain incidents and characters (Winnie and Sam, for instance, do not appear at all and most of the scenes with Aunt Ada's family are left out). The novel, presumably for censorship reasons, is softened at times: at the beginning, Arthur spills beer, rather than vomits, over the elderly couple, and Brenda's gin-and-hot-bath abortion is unsuccessful (and, of course, unshown), leading her to keep the child. None the less, it does create the squalid atmosphere effectively and possesses a still powerfully raw aggression. Albert Finney is astonishingly con-vincing as Arthur and the film created enough shock waves with its treatment of illicit sex for it to be banned in Warwickshire!

Surprisingly, *The Loneliness of the Long-Distance Runner* (1962), directed by Tony Richardson and starring Tom Courtenay as Smith and Sir Michael Redgrave as the Governor, is the longer film (by twenty minutes) and herein lies its main weakness. The story is unnecessarily extended to include a seaside affair with a girl picked up in a stolen car and an interview with a psychiatrist, and contains a number of now dated directorial tricks, involving whirling trees and skies, images shown upside down and the singing of *Jerusalem*. The necessary flashbacks create a disjointed effect and there are obvious problems in attempting to turn someone's often random thoughts into a film. Despite all this, the film does have its strengths: the camerawork creates effectively depressing pictures of drab Midland streets and grey country landscapes; the film is uncompromising – in a way that the ending of the film *Saturday Night* is not – and has the authentic voice of working-class protest; and, above all, Tom Courtenay's deeply felt and intense portrayal of Smith as a sullen, lonely, non-conformist, inarticulate rebel is both powerful and persuasive.

Both were popular and fashionable films and they do succeed in capturing the flavour of the times. Possibly because they are interpretations neither has the power nor hard, grating edge of Sillitoe's original texts.

Reviews and reactions

Saturday Night and Sunday Morning

'His writing has real experience in it and an instinctive accuracy that never loses its touch. His book has a glow about it as though he had plugged in to some basic source of the working-class spirit.'
Manchester Guardian, November 1958.

'Alan Sillitoe stands out because he grew up in a Nottingham slum and writes about the things he knows.'
Books and Bookmen, October 1958.

'For the first time, English working-class life is treated . . . as a normal aspect of the human condition and as natural subject matter for a writer.'
Anthony West, *New Yorker*, September 1959.

'It is in these respects, when he is amoral, unscrupulous and selfish, that he typifies a large section not only of young Nottinghamians but of the youth of Britain today . . . Mr Sillitoe has successfully captured a whole class, the working-class of Britain in the post-war era.'
Nottingham Guardian Journal, October 1958.

'. . . it is impossible not to like this proletarian Don Giovanni; he has the charm of a naughty dog. When it transpires that he has only been sowing wild oats and he settles down abruptly at the end, it is a deep relief to feel that he is going to be adequately protected . . . The style is effectively clear and blunt, as if it has been written with a carpenter's pencil on wallpaper.'
Maurice Richardson, *New Statesman*, October 1958.

'It is good to be reminded that a realistic picture of existence can also be a cheerful one.'
Anthony West, *New Yorker*, September 1959.

On the film: '. . . apart from the actual story that the film tells, it undoubtedly creates the impression that the young men of our cities are a lot of ill-behaved, immoral, drunken teddy-boys.'
Lt.-Col. J. K. Cordeaux, MP for Central Nottingham, *Central Nottingham News*, February 1961.

'Perhaps it would be an overstatement to say that he [Arthur Seaton] was an average type though it is unquestionable that there are many like him in almost any city today.'
Revd Robert Neill, *Yorkshire Post*, February 1961.

'Anyone who thought he was advocating the Arthur Seaton way of life (booze, sex and money) was mistaken. What he was doing was deploring the state of society that forces an Arthur Seaton to lead such an "unsatisfactory life".'
Nottingham Evening Post, September 1961.

'. . . the Rev. John White . . . recommended church people to read Alan Sillitoe's novel, *Saturday Night and Sunday Morning*.
I have read it. It made me vomit. I consider it a foul blot on the fair name of Nottingham.' Letter to the *Nottingham Guardian Journal*, October 1962.

'A mother is going to protest to local education authorities over the setting of part of the novel, *Saturday Night and Sunday Morning*, as homework for her daughter, aged 13.
Mrs Weston said yesterday: "I was disgusted when I saw what she had been given. It is not fit for a young girl to read."'
Daily Telegraph, September 1967.

The Loneliness of the Long-Distance Runner

'. . . there is a very useful kernel nestling at the heart of Smith's story. It is the simple stating of just how outside an Outsider can get. How distantly anti-social. How impossible to coerce, or lure back. How no Borstal in the world can hope to re-do or undo in five years what has taken a boy's whole life to build up.'
Dee Wells, *Sunday Express*, September 1959.

'Like his first book, *The Loneliness of the Long-Distance Runner* is remarkable for its faithful portrayal of working-class folk in Nottingham.'
Nottingham Guardian Journal, September 1959.

'A local atmosphere as pungent as a Trent Valley fog gives Alan Sillitoe's latest book . . . a special significance for Nottingham readers.'
Nottingham Evening Post, September 1959.

'Alan Sillitoe . . . doesn't moralise, or recommend, or view with alarm. He simply reports what he knows, what he has seen, and lends his voice (not as a plea-maker, but simply a story-teller) to those who are so blinded and so choked by their own personal, futile rage that they have no voice of their own.'
Dee Wells, *Sunday Express*, September 1959.

Saturday Night and Sunday Morning

Plot summary

The novel describes episodes in the life of a young Nottingham man, Arthur Seaton. At the start of the novel (he is aged twenty-one), he is in a pub, and, having been in a drinking match with an ex-sailor, he is very drunk. After vomiting over a middle-aged couple, he leaves the pub and goes to the home of Brenda, a married woman with whom he is having an affair. He stays the night as her husband is away.

During the week Arthur works as a capstan lathe operator (a lathe is a machine for shaping metal) in a bicycle factory. He earns the good wage of £14 a week; work is monotonous, though, and he spends most of his day formulating his opinions about life. Brenda's husband, Jack, works at the same factory and tells Arthur he is going to start working nights. Arthur takes advantage of this and sees Brenda three times a week. One evening they make love in the woods and are about to enter the Athletics Club when Arthur notices that Jack is already in the club. Arthur sends Brenda home, concocting a lie for her as to why she is not in the club (as she had told Jack she would be), and drinks with the worried Jack. Arthur feels happy with life.

This mood is dispelled one Friday night when Brenda tells him she is pregnant and the child is definitely his; she wants an abortion and Arthur promises to arrange it for her.

Arthur visits his Aunt Ada who has fourteen children of her own; she advises that Brenda should take a very hot bath and drink hot gin. Arthur spends the rest of the day unfairly winning money at cards from his cousins before he goes out drinking with his cousin Bert, hoping, but failing, to pick up 'tarts'.

The abortion takes place. As well as Arthur, Brenda's friend Em'ler is present. The scene, sordid and tense, culminates in Brenda passing out. Jack returns home unexpectedly, but Em'ler manages to prevent him from coming into the house until Arthur has slipped out of the back door. Arthur goes to the nearest pub where he meets Brenda's sister, Winnie. She is married to a military policeman who is due back in Nottingham the following night. Despite this, she goes to bed with Arthur that night.

A week later we find that the abortion has been successful. At work, Jack warns Arthur that he is being looked for by Bill, Winnie's husband, and his friend from the military police, as Bill has found out about Arthur and Winnie. Arthur tells everything to his brother, Fred, and they go out drinking.

Arthur drinks heavily and gets into a fight in one pub. On leaving the pub, Fred and he witness a drunk man throwing a beer glass through an undertaker's window; the drunk is apprehended by two women and then arrested, much to Fred and Arthur's disgust. On the way home, Arthur is hit by a car. The driver, who is drunk, gets out of the car, only to pass out after being threatened by Arthur. Fred and Arthur turn over his car.

Arthur suspects Mrs Bull, the local gossip, is to blame for his affairs being revealed to the soldiers. So, when off work with a stomach upset, he shoots her with an air-gun. He goes to the pictures with Fred and, on the way out, sees Brenda for the first time since the abortion. He arranges to meet her the following evening. On returning home, Fred and Arthur are confronted by Mr and Mrs Bull about the shooting. Fred tries to placate them but Arthur threatens them with the gun, and they depart amidst much uproar. A policeman comes, but Arthur has hidden the gun and the policeman decides the incident has been no more than an exaggerated neighbours' quarrel.

The novel then moves on four months to August. Arthur spends an evening in the countryside with Brenda prior to his leaving for two weeks of military training. He spends every night of the fortnight drunk, so much so one night that he is unable to get out of bed the next day. On returning to Nottingham he unexpectedly meets Brenda and Winnie in a pub. Brenda is unfriendly and Arthur suspects the women of being there to pick up men. He leaves them and goes to another pub where he meets nineteen-year-old Doreen. He arranges to take her to the cinema the following night. On the way home he sees Winnie again; he walks her home, looking forward to a night of passion.

For three weeks Arthur sees all three women. The Goose Fair arrives and he takes Doreen on the Thursday night and Brenda and Winnie on the Saturday. He is happy and excited on the Saturday night until, on arriving at the bottom of the Helter Skelter, he is confronted by Jack, Bill and Bill's soldier friend. Bill lunges at Arthur who kicks him and makes his escape. At work the next Friday, Jack warns Arthur to settle down. In the course of their awkward conversation, Arthur says he will be drinking in the White Horse that night.

The only person he knows on arrival at the White Horse is his scrounging Uncle George. He decides to have an early night, but, on leaving the pub, is set upon by the two soldiers. He puts up a brave fight but is beaten almost senseless. He staggers back to the pub where he sees Doreen before he collapses.

Having been taken home by Doreen, he spends three days half asleep. In all he takes a week off work. When Doreen visits him, after initially lying to her, he tells her the truth about what has happened to him. He promises not to see Brenda and Winnie again.

Some weeks after returning to work, Arthur meets Jack. He realizes Jack must have told the soldiers where he was drinking the night they beat him up. Jack warns him that Bill is still looking for him. Arthur says he looks forward to the encounter.

That Friday night is 23 December. Arthur takes home a wage packet of £30. Next day he buys presents for his family and goes to spend Christmas at Aunt Ada's. Christmas Eve and Christmas Day are lively and very alcoholic. Christmas ends with one of Arthur's cousins, Jane, splitting her husband's forehead open with a beer glass. Despite this, for the first time since his beating, Arthur feels he is living life to the full again.

Time moves on to March. Arthur is now Doreen's 'young man'. After visiting the cinema one Saturday night, Arthur insists on going for a drink. In the pub he meets Bill. Arthur asks him if he wants to go outside 'for trouble', Bill declines and Arthur buys him a drink. Arthur and Doreen return to her mother's home for supper. They wait, seemingly endlessly, for Mrs Greatton to read the paper and go to bed. When she finally retires to bed, Arthur pretends to leave but does not. Whilst cuddling Doreen he tells her he would like to live with her and look after her. It is a moment of commitment. The novel ends with Arthur fishing by the canal, thinking about life and his forthcoming marriage to Doreen. He is happy, but knows he will always be a rebel.

Critical commentary, textual notes, assignments and GCSE questions

Chapter 1

The first chapter is a memorable one, immediate, glaring and shocking in its impact. It establishes the sordid nature of the novel and the night-time world of the characters. We are introduced to the theme of pleasure taken to excess, even at the expense of others, and to the main axis around which the plot revolves, the adulterous affair of Arthur and Brenda. We gain a striking initial impression of Arthur: reckless, uncaring, outrageous, unapologetic, competitive, successful (in the drinking match and with Brenda), excessive, self-centred and careless of the feelings and thoughts of others.

He laid eight half-crowns on the table, intending to fork out for his own Arthur's relative affluence and his extravagance with money are made clear. Throughout the novel, he is able to look after himself and never relies on others. Each half-crown = 12½p, but was worth much more then.

Piled-up passions were exploded on Saturday night . . . The metaphor 'exploded' effectively creates the weekday feelings of tension and frustration and the violent effect as suppressed passions are given free rein on Saturday nights.

he looked like a tall, thin Druid about to begin a maniacal dance An unusual simile which both suggests the way in which this world of Saturday night drinking is similar to pagan rites being performed and shows how the alcohol leads to a complete lack of control and to dangerous ('maniacal') irrationality.

Too tight Too drunk (slang).

A high-octane fuel of seven gins and eleven pints Again, this metaphor suggests the potentially explosive nature of Arthur Seaton's lifestyle.

a situation of extreme peril Notice how Arthur thought nothing of falling down a flight of stairs, but only worries when he feels his pleasure is to be restricted.

Looks like one of them Teddy boys, allus making trouble Teddy boys (originally so called as they affected a style of dress held to be characteristic of the reign of Edward VII) were viewed as a symbol of rebelliousness in the 1950s. Arthur is not a Teddy boy, but his uninhibited and unapologetic behaviour makes him similarly rebellious.

The beast inside Arthur's stomach ... an appalling growl An appropriate metaphor as Arthur's behaviour is, at times, primitive and seemingly unaffected by the conventions of society.

drop him one Hit him hard enough to make him fall over (colloquial).

duck Colloquial term of endearment.

It was ten o'clock ... Time has now moved on to the next morning. Novels of the 1950s did not generally contain explicit descriptions of sexual activity.

Of all the liars, you're the biggest I've ever known Brenda's assessment of Arthur highlights his unprincipled character, and his pleased retort shows that he is unbothered by conventional standards of behaviour. His pride in lying is one area where he is very similar to Smith in *Loneliness*, who boasts that he can lie 'forever without batting an eyelid'.

an alertness that transformed her face to temporary ugliness This change in Brenda as she hears her husband approach might be viewed as symbolic of her relationship with Arthur; maybe she realizes how sordid and ugly their illicit affair is.

Assignments

1 Write another episode in Arthur Seaton's life.

2 Imagine you are Brenda. Either (a) write her private diary entry for that weekend, not only saying what she did, but expressing her thoughts and feelings as well, or (b) write a letter from Brenda to her closest friend in which she discusses her life, her marriage and her affair with Arthur.

Chapter 2

The chapter is the longest in the novel and, in its contemplative nature, it contrasts with the lively opening chapter. We gain a fuller appreciation of Arthur's character. He is happy, feels himself lucky, stands up for himself and has a sense of fun and devilment, but he is also thoughtful about life and has firm beliefs to which he adheres. He is able to spend many hours formulating his beliefs because of the nature of his job, and it is the establishing of Arthur's working conditions which is of most importance in the chapter. Sillitoe draws on his own experience of working in such a factory and makes clear to us the mono- tonous, dreary and unfulfilling nature of the work. His accurate and detailed descriptions of factory life help to create the 'realistic' feel of the novel and to explain Arthur's excessive behaviour in the previous chapter, which might be seen as a reaction to the boredom of his working days.

now that Arthur had left the bed Though Arthur now earns a good wage, life has not been easy for him and we are constantly reminded of this, here by the fact that he has to share a bed with his brother Sam.

the big grind was starting all over again The monotony of Arthur's work is important; it goes a long way to explaining his desire for excitement and danger in his non-working hours.

taking words out of the air for sport, ready to play with the consequences of whatever he might cause Even when speaking to his father, Arthur seeks to provoke a reaction. Rarely does he think before he speaks, mainly because he has no fears of the consequences of what he says.

the Medders The Meadows: the traditionally poorest area of Nottingham in which the Seatons live.

'I swung the lead and got off 3C,' he added proudly To swing the lead is to malinger, to pretend illness in order to escape duty. Arthur's character is obviously partly explained by the manner in which he has been brought up. His father is proud to have avoided military service; in a family where life has never been less than hard, self-preservation is ranked much more highly than patriotism. '3C' is the category in which Mr Seaton is placed at his medical for the army; it is a category which means he is unfit for military service.

some monstrous being . . . permeated the air The bicycle factory is a life-giving force to Arthur (it pays his wages) and yet it is grotesque, ugly and unnatural. It is a monster from which Arthur is relieved to escape at weekends.

Now, and about time . . . a string of conkers on piece-work The 1950s is often seen as a decade of affluence, as for the first time the working classes began to earn good money. They had to work hard, though, as shown in the vivid metaphor here, suggesting all fat is worked away and the vertebrae of the spine protrude like 'a string of conkers'. 'Piece-work' is where you are paid according to how much you produce.

it was no use saving your money . . . H-bomb on Moscow An important theme: Arthur's extravagance and living for the moment is partly a result of a pessimism and insecurity brought about by the nuclear threat in this decade of brinkmanship (see p. 3 of The fifties . . .)

Billy Graham An internationally popular American evangelist preacher.

never-never Payment by hire-purchase.

snap Colloquial word for food, usually sandwiches, taken to work as a packed lunch.

an air in which pimples grew . . . would have turned you into one big pimple Not only is this literally true, but it symbolically points out the destructive and unpleasant nature of the factory. It creates nothing positive: physically, the air is so putrid the workers get spots and, mentally, it only causes frustration and boredom.

feeding pigs on cherries, as mam used to say — which is something else against my principles Not only does this clearly show the Seaton family's contempt for those in authority, but it is a good example of how, in mid-sentence, the narrative sometimes changes from a third-person description of Arthur to a first-person narration as we begin to read Arthur's thoughts. This technique allows us to know Arthur intimately, but keeps him at a distance; this is one of the reasons why we feel less sympathy for him than we do for Smith in *Loneliness*.

wool-gathering Colloquial expression for day-dreaming, when thoughts are likely to be random, imprecise and woolly.

'Udge up' Budge up: to ask someone to move in order to make more room.

Mostly I'm lucky . . . sometimes I get a smack between the eyes. Not often though In contrast to Jack, Arthur is a risk taker. He gambles with life. It is significant that he spends a good deal of money betting on horses.

I said I was as good as anybody else in the world . . . And I mean it Arthur represents the burgeoning self-respect of the working classes in the 1950s. He knows his worth and intends to live life as he wants, on his own terms.

that's what all these looney laws are for, yer know: to be broken by blokes like me Again, we see Arthur's anti-authority stance and his lack of fear at breaking society's rules. Jack's response to the news that Arthur voted when under the age of twenty-one (the legal limit in 1958) shows how, in contrast, he is law-abiding and fears authority.

screaming abdabs Wild attack of nerves.

feeling as though your arms and legs had been stretched to breaking-point on a torture-rack An appropriate image to sum up the effects of working in the factory.

It was marvellous the things you remembered while you worked on the lathe Notice the use of the second person here; it is as if we are being included in what is being said and has the effect of drawing us further into the world of the novel.

Don't let the bastards grind you down Arthur's motto, summing up his refusal to be dictated to by those in authority.

I couldn't care less if the world did blow up tomorrow Like Smith in *Loneliness*, Arthur is far more concerned with the everyday problems of his own life, than with such major world problems.

Everybody's happy. It's a fine world sometimes, if you don't weaken Arthur's recurring, but changing, thought shows the way in which fortunes change – though it also emphasizes the importance of never weakening (the one part of the expression which does not change).

A terror to men like Jack . . . on the point of breaking out The different ways in which the two men regard Robboe points to a major difference between them: Jack always feels inferior, Arthur never does and, indeed, often feels superior. Arthur is very much in the vanguard of the social revolution which the increased affluence of the 1950s brought about.

rubbers Condoms (slang).

one of the rules of his game As Smith does in *Loneliness*, Arthur views life as a game; like Smith, it is a game he is only prepared to play by his own set of rules.

For Arthur, in his more tolerant moments . . . man's own pleasure Arthur's attitude to women might seem sexist and patronizing today, but was liberal in terms of the attitudes of his day. He does not take women for granted (as Jack does); in recognizing their rights and seeking to give them pleasure, rather than simply taking it from them, he is again radical in his thoughts in going against the conventionally held, if here absurd, beliefs of his day.

Assignments

1 Arthur expresses many views on life in this chapter. Comment on these views and say whether you agree or disagree with them.

2 Compare and contrast Jack and Arthur in this chapter. Which character do you prefer?

3 Arthur feels he is lucky. Do you feel he is lucky? Give reasons for your answer.

Chapter 3

This chapter clearly points out the clandestine and sordid nature of the adulterous affair. One suspects that Arthur is mainly interested in the sex and that Brenda feels the need for some loving (further suggested in the chapter by Jack's lacklustre and lifeless nature). All the main characters are developed and Arthur's belief that he is lucky seems to be substantiated. We certainly see that he is quick-witted, brazen-faced and self-satisfied.

Indian brandy Remedy for stomach ailments.

Bill Hickock Usually known as 'Wild' Bill, he was an American frontier gunfighter of Wild West days.

With a silk scarf covering his windsor-knotted tie Arthur's high self-regard is reflected in the way he dresses: expensively and fashionably.

He wanted all her troubles . . . throw them away Arthur's reaction to life's problems is to ignore them. Without responsibilities, he sees life as easy. As the novel progresses, he comes to realize that troubles cannot always be thrown away.

excitement at doing something she considered not quite right Though Brenda is far less at ease with the affair, her reasons for continuing are not dissimilar to Arthur's: it provides pleasure, excitement and risk in a life of drab monotony.

the delight that a man and a woman generate between them on an overcoat in the darkness However short-lived, however simple, however primitive, however sordid, both Arthur and Brenda require physical pleasure, possibly to make up for their mental boredom.

batchy Stupid (colloquial).

Arthur had once reckoned-up the darts scores . . . very much to Arthur's advantage Even at darts, Arthur cheats; this does not worry him at all: he likes to win and does not care how he does it.

the mask of anxiety Jack is a man seemingly permanently worried, possibly because, unlike Arthur, he is burdened by marital and financial responsibilities.

the fish bite like hungry niggers A coarse and insensitive simile, typical of Arthur with his 'I'm All Right, Jack' attitude. The word 'nigger' was still commonly used in the 1950s.

chops Jaws (slang).

feeling good and generous . . . it's hard luck that things stay the way they do Arthur feels very little remorse or guilt about deceiving Jack; he is happy to put the situation down to luck. He genuinely believes he is one of life's winners and Jack is one of life's losers.

straying too close to the side of the lane, he tripped over a tree-root At this moment of extreme happiness, Arthur trips. Though it means little to him, we might view it symbolically, hinting at the fall he will take when the affair is discovered. Note the similarity with *Loneliness*, when Smith trips when running in full flight.

Assignments

1 Imagine Jack has gone to the club to confront Arthur. Write out, as a short story or play, the ensuing discussion or argument between the two men.

2 Taking into account what you know of their characters, write a scene from a play involving Jack and Brenda in their house.

3 What do you think of Arthur's behaviour throughout this chapter? Is he simply to be condemned or do you see any praiseworthy qualities in him?

Chapter 4

The chapter is one of changing moods. We see Arthur's relative affluence and we are also reminded of the violent world in which he lives. The chapter ends with the ironic juxtaposition of the scenes with William and Brenda. In the former, we see Arthur's fondness for and ease with children – he likes and is liked by William; in the latter, we see his selfishness and insensitivity as Brenda reveals she is carrying his child. Arthur's overriding reaction is one of suppressed annoyance. The chapter marks a turning point in the novel, as we begin to see Arthur's happy and carefree manner resulting in distressing consequences.

the small windows placed high up along the wall were too black to show much daylight Sillitoe constantly emphasizes the unpleasant and depressing working conditions at the factory, making it ever more clear why Arthur seeks excitement away from work.

no strong cause for open belligerence existed as in the bad days At the same time, he points out how much things have improved since the war for the workers; at least now they are able to earn a good wage.

The mother laid a special pay-day treat of bacon-and-beans before them A reminder of the relative austerity of the Seaton family's lifestyle, despite their increased affluence. The pleasures of the household are simple, others being cups of tea and the television.

Goose Fair Fun Fair. Takes place in Nottingham every October.

tick Credit (slang).

inflame the wound An important metaphor at this stage of the novel as, for the first time, a wound has been caused and it is to be greatly inflamed.

those fates that had the power ... whatever it was even worse Arthur believes in making the most of life, but is aware that things do happen that are out of his control and, like Smith in *Loneliness*, he feels that the intervention of fate is rarely beneficial.

'And it's your fault . . . You never will take any care when we're doing it' Arthur's carelessness in sex is symbolic of his careless attitude to life.

Hope to the very end . . . flames are searing your guts Even on hearing bad news, Arthur is hopeful. Throughout the novel, he never feels he is beaten.

I don't feel bad at all. It's an act of God, like a pit disaster One of Arthur's least appealing traits at this stage is his refusal to accept responsibilities; he never blames himself for his actions. He accepts Brenda's 'bad news', but does not readily accept his responsibility as the cause of the situation.

frenchie Condom (slang). The novel is, of course, set in a pre-AIDS era.

bob Shillings (slang). Thirty-five 'bob' is equivalent to £1.75 although worth much more then. Brenda's lack of even this small amount shows what a financial struggle her life is.

Her laugh went echoing bitterly along the empty road, leaping over the dark houses Brenda's unwanted pregnancy introduces the first note of genuine unhappiness to the novel. Arthur might make light of the situation; Brenda is bitter and acrimonious: the 'bit of love' that gave her relief from her difficult and tedious life has resulted in disaster for her.

He still could not worry with her and take it seriously Arthur's carefree attitude is seen at its worst here. His main feeling in this scene is displeasure at the spoiling of his Friday night: it is an ugly, selfish and childish reaction.

Assignments

1 Write a short story, including at a critical point the sentence: 'Her laugh went echoing bitterly along the empty road, leaping over the dark houses.'

2 Arthur's and Brenda's happiness is marred by her pregnancy. Recount a time in your life when a period or moment of happiness was marred for some reason.

3 Do you find yourself liking or disliking Arthur Seaton in this chapter? Look at events throughout the chapter before coming to your conclusion.

Chapter 5

Arthur is genuinely worried for the first time. Only when cheating at cards does he resemble his usual cocksure self. Aunt Ada's family represent the aggressive and anti-establishment nature of this society. The man in the gutter is helped not out of kindness, but to prevent him being arrested: it is done to spite authority. The unprincipled and opportunistic nature of Arthur is shown by the stealing of the wallet.

uncouth suburbs . . . turgid Trent . . . dank air Notice how Sillitoe immediately creates a depressing air to this serious chapter by his use of adjectives.

on the tub, up the stick, with a bun in the oven All are slang expressions for being pregnant.

People make too much about useless things, but you have to get caught by it This shows Arthur's selfish set of values: we might not be surprised at Brenda's concern and do not feel she is making too much of the situation. Arthur does not realize to what extent he will be caught up in the situation.

the Tribe Arthur's word for Aunt Ada's large family.

'Has owd Blackclock bin on to her again?' Aunt Ada is referring to Arthur's father, presumably called 'Blackclock' because of his bad temper ('clock' is a slang term for 'face'); 'bin on to her' suggests that in the past he has beaten his wife.

Ada's three sons . . . from glasshouse and gaol Ada's family, criminals and deserters, are not dissimilar in their disregard for law and authority to Smith in *Loneliness*. 'Glasshouse' is a military prison.

his first wife died of consumption . . . blood-spitting track Increasingly, we are made aware of the toughness and harshness of life as the novel takes on a more serious tone. 'Consumption' is tuberculosis, from which Sillitoe himself suffered.

the Redcaps Military Police.

Arthur dealt the cards . . . without them seeing Again, in the poker game, we see Arthur cheating and winning; he may be lucky but, on occasions, he creates his own luck by cheating.

Chapter 6

This is one of the most disturbing chapters in the novel. The abortion scene is ugly and sordid and in it Arthur's inability to cope with suffering is clearly shown. Em'ler, Brenda's 'touched' friend, is far more useful and does show genuine feelings for Brenda. Arthur's meeting and consequent coupling with Winnie provide him with welcome relief from his troubles; this merely adds to the sour taste in the reader's mouth as it compounds the squalidness of the whole chapter. It is another example of Arthur living only for the moment; like Smith in *Loneliness*, he does not worry about long-term consequences.

touched Mentally retarded or deranged (slang).

rattle Meaningless talk (slang).

No more bubble-baths for Brenda. Never again. I'd rather cut my throat A rare show of remorse and guilt by Arthur. One suspects, though, it is only caused by the ugliness and grotesqueness of the crude abortion attempt.

He was only real inside himself A quotation which exemplifies well Arthur's self-centredness; he is only able to see things from his own viewpoint.

'It's not right, though . . . Men think they can get away with murder' Em'ler sums up the chauvinistic attitude shown by men throughout the novel: they treat women as objects to be used and manipulated. There is little sense of the equality of the sexes.

Arthur, watching from behind, thanked God that Em'ler had done all this It is significant that Arthur himself does little but look on in this scene; it is his carelessness which has brought about the situation, but he does not want to become involved in the ensuing unpleasantness.

his troubles weighing less since he was no more face to face with them Arthur, in his carefree and uncaring manner, is easily able to shrug off troubles. He felt disturbed whilst watching Brenda suffer, but puts this suffering out of his mind as he seeks pleasure for himself.

a slit-trench A narrow trench for a soldier or weapon. This metaphor suggests that Arthur is not able to shrug off completely the unpleasant scene, but that it does remain in his mind.

It's her fault . . . The stupid bloody woman A clear indication of Arthur's inability to be self-critical; his superficial and annoyed reaction to the situation further suggests that he has few real feelings for Brenda and that he has merely been using her for his own gratification.

the man . . . hit the singer, dealing him a violent crack This otherwise insignificant incident serves to heighten the sense of violence which is never far from the surface in the novel.

if the house's scruffy he'll have a fit and black my eyes Violence again rears its head as Winnie reveals herself to be the third wife physically maltreated by her husband (Arthur's mother and sister, Margaret, are the others).

tabs Ears (slang).

Never had an evening began so badly and ended so well, he reflected, peeling off his socks Arthur's unattractive selfishness and the ups and downs of life are both illustrated in this sentence.

Assignments

1 Assess the role of Em'ler. Why does Sillitoe introduce her into the novel? Is she simply 'touched' or does she, at times, speak sense?

2 Examine the ways in which Sillitoe creates mood and atmosphere in this chapter and say how, as a result, you respond to the events in it.

Chapter 7

The chapter is a tense one of violence and potential violence. Arthur's 'luck' might be seen as changing; he is definitely less confident and his outbursts of violence can be seen as reactions to the frustrations and worries of his life. Both the dart landing in his leg and the car running him over might be viewed as symbolic of the change in his fortunes. The drunk who throws the glass through the window adds a further sombre note to the chapter. He is a pathetic figure seemingly crushed by society. The reactions of the crowd reflect the hostile feelings towards authority so often found in the novel. Unlike this pathetic figure, Arthur is still full of fight and no little fury: the turning over of the car might be seen as symbolic of his continued determination to defy the rules of society. By the end of the chapter, he has regained his usual buoyancy of spirit.

swaddies Soldiers (slang).

Jack almost looked at him, but couldn't quite fix his gaze Typical of Jack's timidity and weak character. Even when warning Arthur, he has not the strength of character to look him in the eye.

spoiling the fangs and blunting the claws of his existence Appropriate images for Arthur, who tends to live his life like a wild, predatory animal. Society does tame him, though, to some extent during the course of the novel. At the same time, one feels an untamed and potentially dangerous streak remains throughout.

He did not like to fight ... only the stupid fought with their fists Arthur is prepared to fight, as shown later in the chapter, but he is marked out by his intelligence which helps him to achieve what he wants without resorting to violence. He has the ability to use his brains before his fists, unlike Winnie's husband, Bill, or his cousin, Dave.

beer-off A place where beer might be bought to be drunk off the premises.

konk. Mind (slang).

threw the beer mug . . . The smash sounded musical and carefree Often in the novel violence represents a release from frustration, anxiety or worry. It is only an immediate and short-term answer to problems, however, and usually results in increased long-term problems.

the ratchet-claws of the trap from his brain This metaphor effectively shows how the drunken man is restricted by society and his social position. He feels, unable even to afford a headstone for his mother's grave, that he is trapped by society and that there is no escape. 'She's a stone . . . a rat-clock.' All are terms of abuse for the woman. The venom with which Arthur speaks here shows his own frustration at this time.

the man was a spineless bastard Typically, Arthur has little sympathy with the drunken man; he himself would never give in so easily.

Fred said he would like to fix his fingers . . . press down hard and kill The frustrations imposed by life and the urge to relieve these frustrations by means of violence are even present in the intelligent and bronchitis-suffering Fred. Possibly here he feels frustrated at the unfairness of society and the pointless arresting of the drunken man.

he felt as if a coal fire had been rammed into the back of his throat An appropriately violent and vivid simile which creates effectively Arthur's sense of shock at being run over.

more buoyant and mirthful and stocked with good spirit than for many months One of Arthur's strengths is his ability not to be submerged by his problems. Rarely is he down for any length of time. His determination to enjoy life is immense.

Assignments

1 Explain the significance of the events of this chapter. What do they tell us about Arthur and the world in which he lives?

2 What do we learn of the character of Fred in this chapter?

3 Imagine you are the man who threw the glass through the window. Write an account of his thoughts leading up to the incident.

Chapter 8

The chapter provides an amusing contrast to the more serious ones which precede it and much of the action is dealt with in broadly comic terms. Arthur has recovered his spirits and gains his revenge on Mrs Bull, viewing the shooting as a kind of rough justice. He continues to seek illicit pleasure with Brenda, and we can compare his high-spirited, risk-taking, trouble-causing manner with the more conciliatory and rational character of his brother, Fred. The chapter is mainly comic because no lasting harm is done and Sillitoe has led the reader to react unsympathetically to the malicious Mrs Bull and, therefore, we laugh at her discomfort rather than feel sorry for her. Even the row at the end is amusing rather than disturbing (as much of the previous violence has been), especially with the traitorously liberal Mrs Robin repeatedly fainting and having to be revived with whisky.

sent to Borstal when a kid . . . he hates everybody's guts Bernard Griffin is a typical product of The Meadows, possibly more similar to Smith in *Loneliness* than Arthur.

Arthur was not a very nice bloke . . . a real bastard Arthur's revenge on Mrs Bull is taken in a particularly brutal and hostile manner; it is an act done merely for self-gratification and even Fred cannot justify it.

'He didn't need to pick on me, a woman who's never done a ha'porth of harm to a living soul' This is an ironic statement creating humour as we know it to be untrue. Mrs Bull can be seen to be both self-deluding and self-righteous. 'Ha'porth' is an abbreviated form of 'halfpenny's worth', meaning she has not done even the smallest harm.

twist Tobacco.

'A kid was drowned in Wollaton Cut . . .' 'Is that all?' In this short interchange, Sillitoe reminds us of the suffering and peril in all people's lives; it means little to Arthur, who is a man concerned only with himself.

Mrs Bull was at the door, rat-tat-tatting like a machine-gun An appropriate simile both in terms of the shooting incident and Mrs Bull's hostile nature.

Mrs Robin fainted again The brawl in this chapter is presented much more comically than previous outbreaks of violence, and this is reflected in the repeated and melodramatic fainting of Mrs Robin.

his fifteen days Every year Arthur has to do fifteen days of military training.

Assignments

1 Write a short story involving Mrs Bull.

2 How do you think Brenda feels about Arthur at this stage? Why does she still want to see him? Do you feel sympathy or dislike for Brenda?

Chapter 9

There is a feeling of boredom to this chapter: life between it and the previous one has been monotonous for Arthur. One senses that he feels his life is going nowhere and that he resents this. His resentment is shown both in his expression of anti-establishment views and in the release of his pent-up aggression during his military training. In many ways it is a depressing chapter, as the reader is affected by Arthur's increasingly listless mood, epitomized by his inability to get out of bed for one whole day. One feels his life will not be the same when he returns to Nottingham.

backyards burned by the sun with running tar-sores . . . dustbins overdue for emptying . . . rusting knockers . . . withering flowers . . . smoke . . . coiled blackly This first paragraph provides an excellent example of how Sillitoe creates a depressing atmosphere by his careful choice of adjectives and his selection of details to describe the scene.

Life went on like an assegai into the blue An assegai is a type of spear and the simile suggests the unchanging nature of Arthur's life: it simply keeps going in a straight line.

only tipped with death . . . a nail-punch into the staring sockets of his eyes Sillitoe, from time to time, subtly reminds the reader of the unstable state of world affairs at the time and the resultant insecurity it causes. The metaphor of the nail-punch here is typically graphic and horrific, befitting the violent world of the novel.

the new year swung its fist . . . the high crest of another wave Another violent image, this time suggesting how little control people have over their own lives. Their lives, it is suggested, are dictated for them.

Living in a town . . . it was difficult to follow the changing seasons The monotony of Arthur Seaton's life is further emphasized: one week, one month, one season is very little different from the next for him. It is little wonder that he seeks excitement.

knowing that by this work he never had to worry where the next meal, pint, smoke, or suit of clothes was coming from These are the only important matters in Arthur's life: they show his interest in superficial pleasures and his lack of ambition.

In the army it was: 'F . . . you, Jack, I'm all right.' Out of the army it was: 'Every man for himself!' It is the belief in such precepts that explains Arthur's selfishness.

The only peace . . . waiting for fish to bite, or lying in bed with a woman you loved In a hectic, aggressive life, here are Arthur's true pleasures and maybe suggest that he does have a more gentle, sensitive side.

a nobble A woman who has promised sexual favours (slang).

You never know the difference between right and wrong . . . you were born for trouble Brenda assesses Arthur astutely; it is, of course, this lack of conventional principles that she finds exciting.

The gladness left him . . . the intention of crushing him There is a sense of depression and boredom in Arthur in this chapter; he seems weary of his life and does not seem to possess the unquestioning confidence of the first few chapters.

What am I? he wondered. A six-foot pit-prop that wants a pint of ale . . . whatever people think I am or say I am, that's what I'm not Arthur's self-assessment is important when we come to analyse his character. He is, as his answer to his own question suggests, a man of simple needs; more than this, however, he is ferociously independent and proud of his individuality. He does not want to be categorized by society.

It gave him a satisfaction to destroy Though he hates the army, military training does give Arthur a chance to alleviate his pent-up frustrations. Destruction implies power, and here Arthur can see himself in control rather than in his usual state of being hounded by convention.

Assignments

1 Assess Arthur's views of military service. To what extent do you agree or disagree with these views?

2 How do you think that Arthur's frame of mind differs in this chapter from the preceding ones? Why do you think this is the case?

3 Examine Sillitoe's use of imagery in this chapter and comment on the effects created by it.

Chapter 10

The split between Arthur and Brenda is deepening; her behaviour in this chapter shows her to be as unprincipled as Arthur and suggests that she has been using him as much as he has her. Their only requirement from one another has been physical love, Arthur to satiate his lust, Brenda to compensate for her inadequate marriage.

Arthur is in a state of flux at this stage of the novel. He is not satisfied with his life, though he is not prepared to change his lifestyle. His meeting with Doreen is the watershed between his past and his future; though he does not realize this is an important turning point in his life. Change is often a gradual process and Arthur's second meeting of the evening with Winnie shows that he is still an opportunist, seeking pleasure and prepared to take risks.

Brenda's gin-and-tonic party Arthur's reference to the abortion shows how he has trivialized it and minimized its importance in his mind.

I didn't get out for a single drink A good example of Arthur's glib and ready lying; it does not matter to him that he is talking to Brenda whom he has professed to love.

writing letters was too much like hard work Arthur only puts effort in at work; in his personal life he seeks only easy pleasures. He never thought to write to Brenda as it would not have given *him* any pleasure.

wanting to lose himself in a waterfall of ale and laughter An effective metaphor to describe the refreshing effect pubs have on Arthur's rather tedious life. The effect of the alcohol takes him out of his humdrum life and he is cheered temporarily by the artificially happy atmosphere.

the intense violence needed to relieve the weight of woman-trouble Like alcohol, violence provides an outlet for Arthur from everyday worries. It allows him to relieve his frustrations – even if it is only a brief and temporary relief.

you could usually get what you wanted ... pick the right sort of woman Arthur's double slice of good luck, in arranging a date with Doreen and meeting the willing Winnie on her own, revives his dwindling spirits and, at the end of the chapter, he is as confident as ever.

Chapter 11

In this chapter, Arthur reaches the peak of his fortunes, as he spends three weeks seeing three different women. His worries disappear and his confidence seems greater than ever. The Goose Fair provides the noise and instant excitement for which he so often craves. He is at his most triumphant as he takes Winnie and Brenda around the Fair, stealing kisses alternately from each of them. And yet this chapter also marks the end of the Saturday Night phase of his life. No sooner does he reach the peak of his fortunes than his luck begins to run out, as first Doreen sees him (a situation which he is able to lie his way out of) and then, more importantly, he runs into the women's husbands. He escapes from the soldiers this time, but we feel that his past is catching up with him.

going out with a single girl . . . the hell that older men called marriage Despite her attractions, Doreen presents a problem Arthur is well aware of: the prospect of marriage.

the pleasure and danger of having two married women had been too sweet to resist Arthur avoids 'the safe and rosy path' with Doreen because of the excitement offered by his liaisons with the two married women: the sense of danger only serves to heighten the pleasure.

his capacity for discretion had deepened The worry caused in Chapter 7 has not resulted in Arthur changing his ways, only in his being more careful. He is hardly discreet, though, at the Goose Fair later in this chapter.

so far the tight-rope neither sagged nor weakened nor even threatened to throw him off balance Tight-rope walking is notoriously dangerous and thus provides an effective metaphor to describe Arthur's way of life.

blow for blow Already Arthur's relationship with Doreen is competitive, involving a battle of wits to gain what each wants. Without realizing it, Arthur is no longer at this stage carefree and ruled only by his own desires.

Arthur rolled them down . . . won simply because he kept shouting loudly that he was born lucky Arthur's winning at rolling pennies is symbolic of his reaching the peak of his fortune in this chapter; having reached the peak (carrying on relationships with Winnie, Brenda and Doreen), by the end of the chapter there is only one way he can go: down.

Sanity was out of reach: they were caught up in balloons of light and pleasure that would not let them go The Goose Fair provides such excitement because it is so different from the everyday world of those who attend it. The metaphor of the balloons is appropriate as balloons, of course, can easily be burst – and the Goose Fair only lasts for three days.

He felt like a king up there with so much power spreading on all sides below him Arthur likes power (as shown by his manipulation of the three women) and this simile shows clearly how, for much of the time, he is striving to rise above the commonplace nature of so much of his life and work.

drawing nearer every second to an ocean of which he would soon form another drop of water . . . that unclean turbulent ocean Sillitoe reminds us of Arthur's basic insignificance (in spite of his confidence and self-belief) in terms of society. The metaphor also clearly conveys the squalid and quickly changing nature of that society. When Arthur reaches the bottom of the Helter Skelter (which itself might be viewed as being symbolic of his chaotic and hectic lifestyle), he does indeed find that ocean to be turbulent as he comes face to face with Jack and the 'swaddies'.

Assignments

1 Arthur Seaton is a risk taker. To what extent do you think a person should take risks in life? You may but need not refer to the novel in answering.

2 'Cheats never prosper'. Do you agree?

3 Have you ever done anything you should not have done and been found out? Recount the episode.

Chapter 12

The chapter marks the end of Part I, *Saturday Night*; it is the climax of the novel as Arthur's luck finally runs out completely. At the beginning of the chapter, he is brazen and unrepentant. He makes a mistake, though, in telling Jack where he is going drinking. The scene in the pub represents the lull before the storm as Arthur is bored and talks about dull things to Uncle George. We are not surprised when the storm breaks in the form of the beating up, and Arthur's physical collapse at the end might be viewed as symbolic of the collapse of his whole style of life in the first section.

a dangerous hand of aces . . . one pitch night the royal flush would stay at the bottom of the pack The image is realized at the end of the chapter. The image is appropriate not only because it was a royal flush Arthur first dealt himself when he cheated Dave and Bert at poker, but because gambling is obviously risky and nobody wins every time.
a couple of hundred quids' worth, a fabulous wardrobe of which he was proud Arthur's pride in his appearance is symbolic of his self-esteem; he dresses well because he feels he is important and should dress well.

To be alone . . . He wanted noise, to drink and make love It is as if on a Friday night, at the end of a week's work, Arthur has to justify the tedium of that work by indulging in physical pleasure.

blood behind his eyes distilled to defiance and a hard-gutted core of self-preservation. The war was on at last At last Arthur is made to pay for his illicit pleasures; he does not lack the ability to fight, though, and his response to the situation (during the fight he spurns a chance to run away) rouses our admiration for his defiant and unrepentant spirit.

feeling the world pressing its enormous booted foot on to his head . . . the dark comfort of grime, spit, and sawdust on the floor At last, Arthur's luck has run out and the 'world' (representative of society and its accepted behaviour) crushes him – at least, temporarily. The images make clear the aggressive nature of life.

Assignments

1 Assess the character of Jack as seen in the novel so far.

2 Imagine the next chapter consists of Arthur's thoughts the next day when he wakes up. Write that chapter.

Chapter 13

In this chapter, we see a changed man. Arthur quickly regains his spirit, but the beating does have the effect of curbing his recklessness and impetuosity. No longer will he think of himself as invulnerable; no longer will he take as many chances. He is genuinely touched by Doreen's concern for him, and it is an important moment when he tells her the truth. By doing so, and by Doreen's calm acceptance of the news, the pair of them are brought much closer together. He is pleased that he is no longer keeping secrets and walking the dangerous tightrope mentioned in Chapter 11; she is pleased to be his confidante and to have become more important to him: Doreen can see the path is now clearer to the engagement she hopes for.

The wheels of change It is emphasized increasingly towards the end of the novel that our lives are not purely in our own hands and that life is ever-changing.

a comb-and-paper The combination can be used as a musical instrument.

the raw edge of fang-and-claw . . . he could not but lose Arthur comes
to realize a number of things whilst recuperating, not least that in his
thoughtless rebelliousness he never had a chance of successfully
defying society. The initial metaphor here sums up well the dangerous
jungle-like nature of the world in which Arthur lives.

the tumultuous lake and whirlpool in his mind Another image taken
from the natural world and one which clearly shows the chaotic state
of Arthur's mind.

'I fell off a gasometer for a bet' One way in which Arthur has not
changed (one suspects that he never will) is that he still lies with ease.

'Don't be mardy' Don't be sullen, peevish (slang).

**he felt like a ship that had never left its slipway suddenly floundering
in mid-ocean** This simile again highlights the fact that Arthur has
suddenly realized that there is much more to life than he previously
considered.

**He felt a lack of security. No place existed in all the world that could
be called safe** Having fallen off the metaphorical tightrope and been
hurt, it is not surprising that Arthur now worries about safety. It
explains his change of attitude towards his relationship with Doreen.
She can offer him the safety which he now wishes he had.

**Brenda and Winnie were out of his reach . . . there was always more
than one pebble on the beach, and more than one field in which
clover grew** Arthur is not a man to give up after a beating; he is
always hopeful. Though his attitudes may change to some extent, he is
still the same man. One suspects that, even if he marries Doreen, he
might not always remain faithful.

When wounded he liked to be alone in his lair Notice again the
comparison of Arthur with a wild animal.

**I am a bit of a bastard, he said to himself, after she's been so nice to
me** This is an acknowledgement of his own shortcomings which
Arthur would have been unable to make in Part I of the novel; the
signs of thought for another person and the self-criticism are both
steps forward in his development as a person.

**'It'd tek more than two swaddies to kill me,' he said with
bravado** Swaddy is a soldier. Though he might be more thoughtful
from now on, Arthur will probably never lack confidence in himself.

Assignments

1 How important is the beating up of Arthur in the novel? What
effects does it have on him?

2 Write an essay or short story entitled *The Wheels of Change*.

Chapter 14

The chapter is almost a short story in itself and does seem to be a digression from the main narrative. However, it shows how Arthur regains his appetite for life and highlights a number of the novel's themes. It shows the simple desires of Ada's family, it points to the practical problems of housing and feeding them all, but most of all it emphasizes the brittle nature of their pleasure and the anger of this class of people which smoulders so close to the surface. Life has been hard for Ada's 'tribe' and, though keen to enjoy themselves, they are always ready to react violently to anything that gets in their way. The barely suppressed violence is shown to break out when Jane badly injures her own husband. At the same time, amidst the chaos and hardship, there is an exuberant sense of camaraderie and defiance about them and a determination to live life to the full which is infectious.

his finger hockled His finger bound up.

'You're too much of a trouble-maker . . . too violent. One day you'll really cop it.' Jack's assessment of Arthur might well be true, though there are signs in the rest of the novel that he will be more careful, more controlled and more caring in future.

'You won't knuckle under, Arthur. If you would, you'd enjoy life.' One of the themes of the novel deals with the importance of *not* knuckling under. It is not a good idea to take on the world head-on and unprotected as Arthur has been doing, but it is none the less important to make the most of one's life and not simply do as one's told. Jack's own obvious lack of enjoyment of life disproves his own theory.

A bet on Fairy Glory in the two-thirty won him twelve pounds This success on the horses is symbolic of Arthur's fortunes improving again. He is a person who will always bounce back.

'He thinks all telegrams are sent by tom-tom' Bert's racist joke at the expense of Sam highlights the insularity and narrow-mindedness of the world of The Meadows. There are a number of similar comments in the chapter: they reflect more on the speakers' limitations than on Sam.

the relaxed powder-barrel of each brain A metaphor which sums up superbly the collective temperament of Aunt Ada's family: it is Christmas and they are relaxed, but like powder-barrels they are always likely to explode. Arthur is not dissimilar. The image highlights the barely suppressed anger of many of the people in the novel (also shown later by Dave in the Lambley Green pub).

Arthur clenched his fists, ready to smash him. Arthur is a different person in Part II, but not to the extent that he is not ready to defend himself with violence.

Arthur . . . coming out of a long mistletoe kiss with one of his ginger-haired cousins As he will always be a fighter, so it seems likely he will always struggle to curb his amorous impulses.

Don't be leary Don't be sarcastic, cynical.

Take yer sweat Take it easy, stop bothering.

Housey-Housey Bingo.

Frank . . . was persuading his fiancée to be sick outside It is by the inclusion of such otherwise insignificant details that Sillitoe creates the atmosphere of the novel; this incident illustrates well this chapter of excess and drunkenness.

feeling strangely and joyfully alive . . . ready to tackle all obstacles . . . to turn on the whole world . . . and blow it to pieces Christmas with Ada's 'tribe' re-kindles Arthur's enjoyment for life and his rebelliousness. His rebelliousness does become more focused than before, though, and tends to be pointed at the government and authority, whereas previously it was expressed simply by defying society's conventions in a random manner as he sought to gain personal pleasure.

Chapter 15

In this chapter, Arthur makes the important decision to marry Doreen: he has opted for security rather than dangerous pleasure. His decision seems to the reader to have been inevitable, mainly because of Alan Sillitoe's skill in developing his character. Arthur remains a liar and a rebel, but both of these sides of his character are now more carefully channelled and controlled. We see (owing to the fact that Sillitoe regularly allows us into Arthur's thoughts) that his decision gives him great pleasure, but that he is also fully aware of its drawbacks. In this decision, one suspects Arthur is not dissimilar to many young men facing up to the daunting prospect of marriage (even if few will have previously lived so 'wildly').

The chapter also ties up the remaining loose end of its structure: Bill. His feud with Arthur, it seems, is now over. The introduction of Chumley into the story is more difficult to explain. One wonders how he became attached to Mrs Greatton. They are an odd couple, possibly reflecting the fact that in life unlikely people are often thrown together by fate for countless reasons which are difficult to explain. Arthur and Doreen themselves do not seem very well matched in terms of temperament and beliefs. In many ways, their marriage is one of mutual convenience, the result of upbringing and past experiences as much as physical and mental attraction.

if you don't stop that bastard government . . . blow their four-eyed clocks to bits This whole paragraph provides a clear indication of Arthur's contempt for authority and his determination not to be taken advantage of.

Your phizzog Face (vulgar form of the word 'physiognomy').

They've got you by the guts, by backbone and skull, until they think you'll come whenever they whistle Arthur realizes the overwhelming power of authority, but the words 'they think' suggest that, like Smith in *Loneliness*, he is not prepared to be completely subservient, to be treated like a tame animal.

I'm a bloody billy-goat trying to screw the world, and no wonder I am, because it's trying to do the same to me An aggressive and appropriate image to sum up Arthur at this stage: billy-goats are kept in captivity (and Arthur is now heading for the restrictions of a steady relationship and eventually marriage), but they remain hostile and are rarely, if ever, fully tamed.

implying: 'But I'll tame you' Sillitoe's choice of words here again presents Arthur as a wild animal; Doreen, though, will not allow him to run free.

jankers Imprisonment or confinement to barracks (army slang).

fighting the last stages of an old battle . . . feeling the first skirmishes of a new conflict Arthur's style of life might have changed, but he knows life will always be a battle for him and that he has simply chosen to fight a different type of battle.

he was good in his heart about it . . . making for better ground than he had ever trodden on before It is important to realize that Arthur feels he is making the right decision; he does feel his life now might be much more worthwhile.

Chapter 16

The novel ends symbolically: Doreen might be viewed as the bigger fish Arthur reels in whereas his adulterous affairs which he has now rejected might be seen as similar to the fish he throws back. This is a positive end to the novel, suggesting that Arthur has made the right decision. He is certainly contented as the novel draws to a close. He knows life will never be easy, but he has now gained security and a greater sense of purpose. He has matured and learnt and might now be in a position to achieve something more lasting than he has ever done before.

his own catch had been made, and he would have to wrestle with it for the rest of his life Not only does this show Arthur's continuing awareness that life will always be a struggle, but it does also show that he feels his marriage with Doreen will be a commitment for life.

'Everyone in the world was caught, somehow . . .' Arthur's realization that it is impossible to be a completely free spirit marks an important development in his character; no longer is he trying to avoid being caught (something bound to failure); but now he aims to make the most of the situation having accepted the bait.

fighting every day until I die . . . trouble it's always been and always will be We are left in no doubt that Arthur will always be a rebel; he may have conformed to some extent by marrying, but we can be sure marriage will not turn him into another Jack.

it's a good life and a good world . . . if you don't weaken Arthur may have modified his lifestyle, but he has never given in. He finishes the novel feeling optimistic about life. As he catches the larger fish in the last sentence, we feel confident he will always win more than he loses.

The characters

Arthur Seaton

I'm a bloody billy-goat trying to screw the world, and no wonder I am, because it's trying to do the same to me

Arthur Seaton dominates the whole novel: he is a man of his times, but by no means a stereotype. He is a complex human being. He is attractive in many ways, but has many failings. Those failings, though, are recognizably human failings. Consequently, we might not like Arthur Seaton (and, at times, it is difficult not to be disgusted by his behaviour), yet it is impossible not to see why he is the way he is, and it would be a harsh judge who would condemn him out of hand. The novel traces his development from twenty-one to twenty-four and during its course his outlook on life changes gradually but perceptibly.

Arthur's weaknesses are often transparent. Alan Sillitoe himself wrote of him (in his autobiographical essay, *The Long Piece*) that he is 'a young anarchic roughneck' and said that there is 'nothing heroic about Arthur Seaton'. He is complacent and self-satisfied: he enjoys his indulgent lifestyle and is so un-selfcritical that he does not feel any guilt at all about Brenda's unwanted pregnancy, declaring it to be an unavoidable 'Act of God'. We know that, in fact, it is his fault because he refused to wear a condom whilst making love to Brenda (as 'Frenchies ... spoil everything'). His self-centred, insensitive lack of concern for Brenda (Chapter 4 tells us he is unable to take the situation seriously) produces a disgust in the reader which is compounded by his unwarranted and unjustified annoyance at Brenda: 'It's her fault ... The stupid bloody woman.' Arthur is a reckless, unprincipled, careless man who seeks fun and pleasure excessively; he takes risks, causes trouble, is unscrupulous, amoral, cunning and hypocritical. He is a liar, indeed he is a master-craftsman of dishonesty. His behaviour is primitive, uninhibited, sometimes outrageous, sometimes callous, and always egotistical. He is high-spirited and cocksure, belligerent, and uncaring of the consequences of his actions. He is destructive by nature and, possibly worst of all, he shirks commitments and avoids responsibilities. In addition to all of this, he is unapologetic and unrepentant about his behaviour and rarely feels any remorse or guilt for the harm he causes.

Examples of these weaknesses abound. His reaction to the pregnancy possibly sees him at his worst; his cheating at poker and darts, his adulteries, his turning over of the car, his vomiting over the middle-aged couple in the White Horse, his violent drunkenness and his self-confessed 'Couldn't care less' attitude show him in no better light. The extent of his failings is such that, in Chapter 8, even his brother Fred has to admit that he is 'a real bastard' and, in Chapter 13, Arthur himself acknowledges 'I am a bit of a bastard'. And yet it is undeniably difficult not to like Arthur Seaton. The Revd Robert Neill, writing in the *Yorkshire Post* in April 1961, declared that on the whole he thought him 'an attractive sort of fellow' and it is difficult to disagree with this assessment. This is because his many weaknesses are both mitigated by his upbringing and environment and counterbalanced by a number of admirable characteristics.

Living in The Meadows and working as a capstan lathe operator at the bicycle factory are not circumstances to induce sensitivity. Arthur has been brought up in a community which loathes the establishment (as witnessed by his Father's 'swinging the lead' to avoid military service and his cousins' desertion and stealing) and it is not surprising that he is disdainful of authority and accepted codes of behaviour. In the first chapter, it is said that he looks as if 'about to begin a maniacal dance' and in Part I of the novel we witness that dance as he defies convention and socially expected norms. This urgent, if unfocused, rebelliousness in his character is further heightened by the numbing monotony of his job which he feels impelled to react against.

Beyond the reasons for Arthur's bad behaviour, however, we also can witness positive traits in his character. He is kind and generous to children (he is obviously much liked by both Brenda's son, Jacky, and Margaret's son, William). He is always confident and optimistic ('Hope to the very end', he declares to himself in Chapter 4) and, at times, we feel he creates his own luck by his determination to succeed. He does not bear personal animosities and, though initially he tries to avoid them, he does accept the consequences of his actions. It is significant that he does not cause trouble when he meets Bill in the pub in Chapter 15. He is adventurous and exciting (probably the reasons why Brenda and Winnie are so readily attracted to him), he has an infectious sense of fun and harmless devilment (witness the hilarious chaos he creates on the Ghost Train at the Goose Fair), he is dynamic, virile and compelling. He is quick-witted and not unintelligent, and is a skilled and hard-grafting workman. He is a charismatic man with a huge and enviable appetite for life ('stocked with good spirit'); he realizes his own worth (staunchly believing he is 'as good as anybody else in the world') and fears nobody.

As the novel progresses, so Arthur's character develops and it develops for the better. One of the main reasons for this is that he gains in self-awareness and comes to appreciate the shortcomings of his earlier lifestyle. The abortion and the increasing discontent he feels in the following months (dispelled only briefly by the outrageous three weeks when he is seeing all three women) begin to bring about this change, but it is his violent beating by the two soldiers which so clearly shows him the dangerous nature of his lifestyle. For a time after this he feels like a ship 'that had never left its slipway suddenly floundering in mid-ocean', but he is intelligent enough to take stock of his life. He realizes sacrifices have to be made and compromises reached; he welcomes the security offered by Doreen and is aware of her worth. He is, at the end, deservedly content because, though he never apologizes for his earlier excesses and indulgences, he makes a conscious effort to curb them and to lead a less selfish life. He has matured, certainly not fully, but he seems set to channel his rebellious urges more constructively. He is determined in the final chapters to focus his rebellious attention on the 'vast crushing power of government' and it is no surprise that Alan Sillitoe said in a 1961 interview (in the *Nottingham Evening Post*) that 'if one were to continue the story of Arthur Seaton ... what he would do about it [i.e. his previous unsatisfactory life] is to become a Communist or a socialist or a trade unionist'.

Indeed, one is bound to feel hopeful for Arthur Seaton because of character traits which do not change in the course of the novel: his indomitable spirit and his ferociously guarded independence. 'Don't let the bastards grind you down,' he declares and we admire his determination that they will not. He may not achieve much in his life, and he takes a beating in the novel, but he is a man whom we feel will never be entirely defeated. He will always be a rebel, defiant and with 'a hard-gutted core of self-preservation'. Apart from in the immediate aftermath of this beating (when he is enveloped temporarily by a 'black cloud of ... melancholy'), he never weakens in his resolve to make the most of life and be his own man. Sillitoe wrote in *The Long Piece*: 'I myself have always lived by the words of Tolstoy's advice to Maxim Gorki: "Don't let anyone influence you, fear no one and then you'll be all right."' The words might well be applied to Arthur Seaton.

Jack

The worried expression returned to Jack's face

Jack is very much a contrasting figure to Arthur. He is uncharismatic, dull and lacks passion. In no way is he a rebel. Whereas Arthur taunts the foreman Robboe, Jack is respectful and scared of him. His philosophy in life is to work hard, think of others and avoid trouble at all costs. On a number of occasions he advises Arthur to calm down and 'knuckle under'. Even when he knows about Arthur's adultery with Brenda he is unable to confront Arthur about it. Instead he finds out that Arthur is drinking in the White Horse that night and informs the soldiers. Although we can appreciate his kindness and thoughtfulness earlier in the novel – he drinks work tea so as not to put Brenda to the trouble of making him a flask and works nights to earn the money to buy Brenda a television – this cowardly incident alienates us from Jack. When Arthur calls him a 'sly spineless bastard' and 'narrow-gutted' in Chapter 14 we tend to agree with him. Jack is not a bad man, but he is too lacking in life. It is not surprising that Brenda is bored with him; he obviously cares for her and works hard to make his family's life easier (and, indeed, he gains promotion during the novel), but he is unexciting and lacks individuality. The only time he seems at all animated is when he talks about Notts. County in the Athletics Club in Chapter 4. The rest of his life he seems to be worried or anxious. Words used to describe him in the novel include: sallow, furtive, frigid, earnest, sad, nervous, shifty, efficient, slow and embarrassed. He is a man barely able to cope with life and he never gains our respect. His inability to face up to life is symbolically shown when he talks to Arthur in Chapter 7: 'Jack almost looked at him, but couldn't quite fix his gaze.'

Brenda

In some ways, Brenda is the saddest figure in the novel. She is trapped in a marriage with Jack and after seven years of the marriage she craves excitement. She knows her affair with Arthur is 'not quite right' but she cannot resist the 'hasty abandonment of making love' as in that abandonment she escapes from the drudgery and monotony of her everyday life. Her 'bit of love', though, leads only to embitterment and disillusionment, as first she becomes pregnant and later the affair is discovered. She disapproves of the wilder side of Arthur's character, realizing he is 'born for trouble', as shown by her unfavourable opinion of his shooting Mrs Bull, and yet she is unable to resist him. She is shown to have more sense than her sister Winnie (witness the different manner in which they roll pennies in Chapter 12), but she is frustrated and not at all faithful. In Chapter 10 it is made clear that she was in The Match to find a man to go home with and she succeeds. That she is like this is due in no small degree to the dullness of Jack (with whom, she tells Arthur in Chapter 4, she has not made love in months); however, she is supported wholly by Jack and is never likely to divorce him. She is trapped, and it is this which makes her such a sad figure: at the end, we feel hers will be a discontented and unfulfilled life.

Doreen Greatton

Brenda provides sexual excitement and danger for Arthur; Doreen, nineteen, attractive yet pale, is not as forthcoming sexually, but offers Arthur security and stability. She provides a direct contrast with Brenda in a number of ways: she is slim, whereas we hear of Brenda's 'bulging breasts' and 'ample lower portions'; she is demanding of Arthur and does not allow him his own way; she does not live in the slums of The Meadows, but on a new housing estate; and her job at Harris's hairnet factory grants her an independence and self-sufficiency so lacking in Brenda. Unlike Brenda she is no pushover for Arthur; she warns Arthur she intends to tame him and we feel he will be in for a hard battle. Her strength of character is suggested in Arthur's initial reaction to her as being a 'still-waters-run deep' woman. It is shown in her calm acceptance in Chapter 13 of his philanderings with Brenda and Winnie and her resolve to marry him.

She is limited in her ambitions and desires. She seeks only marriage and a house. At nineteen she feels left on the shelf and can only envisage her future life in terms of husband and children. Consequently, we see she deludes herself about Arthur and creates her own image of him ('honest and straight'), so determined is she to gain a husband and settle down. She will certainly provide Arthur with a more secure base than he has had before, but one is left wondering at the end how happy or permanent the marriage will be.

Minor characters

The novel abounds with minor characters, playing important cameo roles and adding to the impression that Sillitoe is not just writing about an individual but a whole class of people. These characters, especially those who appear very briefly, are sometimes sterotypes, and all are necessarily sketchily created, but many are intriguing and have their own individuality. All serve a purpose, whether it be to highlight a certain aspect of society or as a means for the plot to function. Many help to throw further light on Arthur's character. The large-breasted, dark, attractive, pliable *Winnie* certainly does this. She has 'the greed of a passionate woman who has been parted too long from her husband' and provides a further outlet for Arthur's sexual desires. This highlights Arthur's lack of restraint and discretion in Part I and his lack of real affection for Brenda. Winnie also serves to show that Brenda is not to be simply condemned for her infidelity; trapped in dull marriages, treated as mere accessories to their husbands, with no other outlets to relieve their frustrations, it is little surprise that the likes of Winnie and Brenda seek solace in the arms of a free spirit such as Arthur.

Other characters

Ada Reflects the ability of the human spirit to triumph over hardship. Despite her fourteen children, her violent and often unemployed first husband, and clashes with authority, she remains unbowed and even in her fifties she is exuberant in her enjoyment of life. *Fred* Possibly because of his bronchitis, he shows an unusual sensitivity in this environment. He is intelligent (witness his ability to talk fluently about the wars in Korea and Libya) and calm (as seen in his dealings with the Bulls in Chapter 8), but even he is so affected by the unfairness of life that in Chapter 7 he feels that he would like to kill someone. *Mrs Bull* A stereotypical gossiper: malicious, hypocritical, self-righteous, domineering and vindictive. Her come-uppance in Chapter 8 provides much humour. *Dave and Bert* Arthur's anarchic cousins who steal beer from the cellar of the pub next door. Bert shows the insular nature of this society in his racist jokes about Sam, and Dave, who deserted from the army, shows its anger in his despising of authority, his hatred of the 'rat-faced whore' he made pregnant and his readiness to fight in the Lambley Green in Chapter 14. *Sam* Calm, intelligent and attractive (witness the number of mistletoe kisses he is subjected to), provides a polite and refined counterpoint to the males of Ada's house. They feel, coming from the Gold Coast and being black, he will be primitive and uncivilized; Sillitoe shows it is the inhabitants of The Meadows who are like this.

There are many other minor characters. There are the henpecked husbands, *Mr Bull* and *Ralph*; the maltreated wives, *Margaret* and *Mrs Seaton*. There are the children, *Jacky* and *William*, who both adore Arthur and are exposed to poor home lives. With the examples they have been set, one would not be surprised if they too grow up to be unprincipled and immoral. We also meet the aggressive, television-watching *Mr Seaton*; the mean, sponging *Uncle George*; the fainting Liberal, *Mrs Robin*; the 'touched' but faithful *Em'ler*; *Jane*, a younger version of Ada, and *Jim*, possibly a younger version of Ralph; the disliked but not unfair member of the management, *Robboe*; the violent soldiers, *Bill* and his friend; and the strict *Mrs Greatton* who, none the less, is living in sin with the uncommunicative, enigmatic '*Chumley*'. All have one thing in common: they are struggling to come to terms with the problems and difficulties of life. And they all help to provide the reader with the feeling that he is experiencing life in a whole society. It is significant that few, if any, of the minor characters are attractive or successful; it is a society in which being tough enough to survive is the main priority.

Themes

In his introduction to the 1979 edition of the novel, Alan Sillitoe wrote: 'I had no theme in my head except the joy of writing.' This may be so and, indeed, *Saturday* contains no explicit judgements or moral preaching by the author. However, in his depiction of working-class life in Nottingham, a number of themes do emerge.

Pleasures and responsibilities

Arthur Seaton starts the novel extremely drunk and spends the majority of the novel seeking pleasure. His concerns are eating, drinking, smoking, clothes and women. He is excessive in his behaviour (in Chapter 1, he drinks thirteen pints and seven gins, vomits over two people, and makes love for an hour to Brenda; by Chapter 11 he is having relationships with three different women) and, with his 'couldn't care less' attitude, he refuses to be restricted by society's conventions. He lives for the moment, declaring in Chapter 2 that there is no point doing otherwise when the Americans might drop an H-bomb on Moscow at any time. He is 'caught up in balloons of light and pleasure' at the Goose Fair, which represents the zenith of his pleasures; it is soon after this that the balloon bursts for Arthur and he has to face up to the consequences. The Revd Robert Neill, the Vicar of Lenton, an industrial parish of Nottingham, summed up the situation well when he wrote in the *Yorkshire Post* in 1961 that Arthur, unexaggeratedly, represents 'a certain type of young lad who had not yet faced up to life and has not considered the consequences of his uncontrolled passions'. The violent beating up of Arthur is, of course, not the only consequence. Earlier, Brenda suffered because of the careless loving of Arthur and herself, and her 'bit of love' results in the bitterness, acrimony and pain of the abortion. Arthur did not learn from this, though, because he personally did not suffer the pain but was inconvenienced only; indeed, afterwards, his behaviour becomes more unrestrained as he finds 'the pleasure and danger of having two married women . . . too sweet to resist'.

Danger and safety

The novel highlights that such pleasures are fraught with danger and do cause hurt. Arthur avoids responsibilities: his reaction to the pregnancy is that he simply wants to throw all of Brenda's troubles away and he feels no guilt about it, dismissing it as an unavoidable 'Act of God'. He is young and probably wants to avoid the hardships and worries he sees in the married lives of his parents, Aunt Ada, Margaret and Jack, the last so burdened with responsibilities that he often wears a 'mask of anxiety'. And yet he is not young enough to ignore his responsibilities. He is not unaware that actions have consequences and in Chapter 2 he happily admits that he has been struck because of his behaviour. But some actions are more serious than others and have to be paid for over a longer time. Arthur realizes over the course of the novel that the pleasures of sin tend to be short-lived and that the excitement caused by danger can also lead to unpleasant repercussions so much greater than the initial pleasure. Brenda too is excited 'at doing something she considered not quite right', but the novel puts the question in our mind as to whether such excitement is ultimately worthwhile. To begin with Arthur rejects the 'safe and rosy path' offered by Doreen, but increasingly he realizes the importance of security and safety. In Chapter 15, as he walks in the countryside with Doreen, he feels little excitement but he experiences a deeper satisfaction in feeling the absence of danger. The novel shows clearly how one has to gauge short-term pleasure against long-term contentment, how one has to weigh up the merits of excitement (and possibly danger) against safety (and possibly boredom) and how one has to realize that actions have consequences and, ultimately, one has to face up to one's responsibilities.

The effect of environment

Arthur is the limited young man that he is, dominated by ephemeral and materialistic pleasures, because of the world he has been brought up in: the slum jungle of The Meadows and the claustrophobic treadmill of the bicycle factory. Alan Sillitoe himself wrote about the novel in 1961 in the *Nottingham Evening Post*: 'It is the story of a man who ... has no spiritual values because the kind of conditions he lives in do not allow him to have any.'

The novel has been hailed as one of the first to deal seriously and genuinely with the lives of the working class, and it does clearly illustrate the frustrations and resultant violence of unfulfilled lives.

Throughout Sillitoe emphasizes the grim and lacklustre nature of Nottingham and we witness an environment that sucks all who exist in it down into the subjection of an unsparing and drab monotony, alleviated only at weekends. Work is unmitigatingly dull and can be tackled without thinking. Arthur refers to it as the 'big grind', and 'the week's monotonous graft' is referred to in Chapter 1. The effect of this is that boredom and frustration are created. Life is so monotonous in this environment that we are told in Chapter 9 that it is difficult to differentiate between the seasons of the year, as life never changes, simply goes on 'like an assegai into the blue'. This lifestyle not surprisingly leads to 'piled-up passions' and Sillitoe describes each member of Ada's family as like a powder-barrel ready to explode. Even the most sensitive character in the novel, Fred, feels the desire to kill after witnessing what he sees as the unfairness of life when the drunken man throws his beer glass through the undertaker's window. That the man is pushed to do this shows the extent of his frustration and Arthur's reaction to the action, feeling the sound of the breaking glass to be 'musical and carefree', illustrates clearly the desire to break the unvarying pattern of life.

Monotony leading to violence

The novel shows how this monotony leading to frustration in turn leads to violence and from this it can be viewed as an indictment of society at the time. Margaret has to stay at her parents' house to avoid being beaten up by her husband; Mr Seaton has in the past mistreated Mrs Seaton; Winnie says Bill will black her eyes if the house is not tidy; Jane hits her husband with a beer glass; in Chapter 6, the singer in the pub is hit because of the poor quality of his singing; Arthur himself hits the unapologetic dart player, threatens the drunken car driver who ran him over that he will 'SMASH' him 'ter smithereens' (both in Chapter 7), is ready to 'smash' the aggressive man in Chapter 14, and enjoys the destruction involved in his military training. All of this, one feels, is the result of the world in which the characters live: the only way they know to relieve their anger and frustration is the 'intense violence' Arthur seeks in Chapter 10. It is a violence born out of a subconscious disgust with their lives.

Restraint and self-control

In a similar way to much of the pleasure gained, the violence in the novel is shown to grant only short-term relief. Though it is never suggested that one should simply give in, it is possibly implied that one should temper one's impulses with restraint and discretion. The most self-controlled character, Jack, is the only one we are told of receiving promotion and Arthur's development as a person is coupled with his increasing self-restraint. We can see this when he neither hits the aggressive man in Chapter 14 nor does he take his opportunity to gain his revenge on Bill in Chapter 15. And the most important relationship of his life, with Doreen, is the one where he had to wait before receiving any kind of sexual favours (we are told of his advances in the cinema being constantly rebuffed by Doreen). We might interpret the novel as showing the long-term advantages of self-control compared with the merely short-term relief granted by impulsive violence.

The working class

That life is hard for the industrial working class is a recurring theme. At home, Arthur has to share a bed with his brother. Work for many requires hard graft (turning 'your backbone to a string of conkers') and is done in depressing places such as the bicycle factory where the windows are so small, dirty and set so high up the wall that little light ever shines through. Ralph's first wife and eighteen-year-old daughter both died of consumption, Fred suffers from severe bronchitis and even Arthur is affected by stomach upsets owing to the environment in which he lives. In 1958, few had written about this sector of society and *Saturday* certainly brought across to many people (as it still does today) the extent to which life is a battle for so many. Even at the end Arthur realizes he will have to fight every day until he dies; and of course, his motto throughout is 'It's a hard life if you don't weaken.'

Fate

As in any stratum of society Fate too has its part to play and, though Arthur believes in, creates and rides his own luck to some extent (for various reasons he wins on the horses, at cards, darts and rolling pennies during the novel), he too is ultimately in the hands of Fate. Luck is always changing, the novel points out, and it is the Fates that have the final say. Arthur can do nothing about the dart ricocheting into his leg or the car running him over in Chapter 7. He realizes, when beaten up, that it is not just the two soldiers but 'the world pressing its enormous booted foot on to his head' and when he wakes up he realizes it is 'the wheels of change that were grinding their impressive tracks'. Sillitoe emphasizes man's inability to dictate his own Fate. Like the fish in the final chapter, we are left in no doubt that none of us is ever able to swim free for ever.

Anti-establishment and rebellious attitudes

In the light of the environment in which they live, it is hardly surprising that many of the characters have an anti-establishment outlook on life. Ada's three sons spend the war deserting from the army and stealing whenever they are not inside a glasshouse or gaol, and Arthur's father is proud of fooling the army medics and being passed unfit for military service. People in The Meadows feel their country has done little for them and that they owe it nothing in return; as Dave puts it, he has no intention of fighting 'for them bastards'. Hatred of authority and defiance of law and order is prevalent throughout the novel. Arthur and Bert only rescue the drunken man from the gutter so that he will not fall into the hands of the police. Arthur is rebellious throughout. Not only is he determined not to let 'the bastards grind' him down, but he flaunts authority at every opportunity: he complains about the tea so much at work in Chapter 2 that it is changed; he votes instead of his father in the same chapter when he is legally not old enough to vote; he wonders at the top of the Helter Skelter whether there are enough people at the Goose Fair for a successful rebellion; he feels after Christmas at Aunt Ada's that he is ready to blow the whole world to pieces; and bemoans the 'bastard government' and feels that they ought to be blown 'to bits' in Chapter 15.

Arthur Seaton is very much an individual, but, on reading the novel, we cannot help feeling that his dissatisfactions represent a whole class of people, not least the author who wrote in the *Sunday Express* in 1970: 'I see society as my enemy because I want to be free.'

Individuality and selfishness

Pride in one's individuality and the desire to preserve it might also be seen as themes of the novel. Arthur fears being classified and says whatever people think he is, that is what he is not (Chapter 9). He can pay his own way in life, asks for nothing from anybody, and is entirely his own man. In Chapter 2 he assures Jack that he knows he is 'as good as anybody else in the world'. He is proud of his 'fabulous wardrobe' of slick suits, expensive ties and shoes, and silk scarf, for he has earned it. And whatever he does he faces up to the consequences (even though he does not tend to think ahead as to what they will be) and by doing so he maintains his self-esteem (unlike Jack who betrays Arthur to the soldiers in order to gain his own revenge). This individuality can also be linked with the sharpened instinct of self-preservation shown by Arthur and with his downright self-centredness. In the first chapter we are told of his 'strong sense of survival' and nowhere is this more strongly seen than in the climatic fight where his 'hard-gutted core of self-preservation' comes to the fore. This is a trait to admire, and one we suspect is necessary to survive in the society of The Meadows, but less admirable is Arthur's lack of concern for others. Abundant examples of this can be found: he tells Jack he does not believe in 'share and share alike'; he only feels 'real inside himself'; and he declares he has no interest in whether the world is to be blown up or not. This selfish attitude is understandable, if not likable. In the jungle of the world of the novel, it is 'Every man for himself' or, as they said when Arthur was in the army: "'F . . . you, Jack, I'm all right.'" Sillitoe does not make explicit judgements, but it is clearly implicit that a society has come about which is most unsatisfactory. He does not criticize those who live in The Meadows (indeed, we tend to admire the way that, though they cannot possibly win, they fail to be bowed by defeat and keep coming back for more) so much as question how their situation has been allowed to come about.

Dishonesty and distrust

The novel also questions the practicality of honesty. Lying, cheating and deceit are rife in the novel, possibly not surprisingly amongst people who distrust the very society in which they live. Arthur is the biggest liar, as Brenda says, and cheat of them all. Occasionally, he is found out, as with his adulteries, but more often than not he benefits from his dishonesty. He wins fifteen shillings off Dave and Bert at poker by secreting cards on his lap; in Chapter 3, he wins at darts by deliberately getting the scores wrong; and, throughout, he placates people by following his motto of 'Lie until you're blue in the face', even to the extent that Doreen is pleased as to how 'honest and straight' he is. He himself is lied to when Brenda cheats on him in Chapter 10. That dishonesty is so much the norm again reflects on the society in which the characters live: it is one of distrust, to such an extent that Arthur even has to hang his coat on a nearby hook at work so that he can keep an eye on his belongings.

Other themes

In a novel of much action and many episodes one can, of course, endlessly suggest themes. We see the sheer inexplicable strangeness of life in the relationship between Mrs Greatton and Chumley; we see patronizing racism shown towards Chumley and Sam; we see the desire for revenge (not just the soldiers on Arthur, but also Arthur on Mrs Bull with the air-gun); we see the plight of women in this society (as Em'ler says: 'Men think they can get away with murder') and also the growing refusal to be completely subservient to men (as shown in different ways by Brenda, Winnie, Doreen, and Jane); and we see how life so often presents dilemmas (danger or safety, pleasure and pain or ease and boredom). And so one could go on. That one can is a tribute to the richness of the novel, for it is not just Arthur Seaton's story but it is the successful representation of a whole class (that which the American playwright Arthur Miller called 'that darkest Africa of our society').

Hope

Many of the themes mentioned are depressing, but, ultimately, the novel is one of hope: it is realistic but not without cheer. 'Hope to the very end,' Arthur tells himself in Chapter 4, and this is true of the whole novel. For whatever the problems of his life, and we know there will be more to come, Arthur has achieved things by the end: he has survived, he has developed, and he knows he is 'making for better ground than he had ever trodden on before'. And, as the novel closes, Arthur believes that 'it's a good life and a good world . . . if you don't weaken'.

Style

Naturalism

Saturday Night and Sunday Morning is a naturalistic novel; it is, as the critic Richard Lester wrote of another Sillitoe novel, *Key to the Door*, 'a rich book which reeks of life, raw, pulsating and intensely lived'. It is set in a real place, The Meadows in Nottingham, and the pubs and streets mentioned in the novel do (or did) actually exist. Sillitoe himself, in his introduction to the 1970 edition, wrote that it mirrored 'the sort of atmosphere that I grew up in'. Constantly we find we can easily believe in his characters. This is not least because of the way Sillitoe makes them speak. He accurately recreates a Nottingham dialect and uses slang to good effect. Examples of this are numerous: Em'ler is 'touched' (Chapter 6), Arthur is 'too tight' and calls people 'duck' (Chapter 1), Dave is on a 'nobble' (Chapter 9) and Aunt Ada asks Arthur: 'Has owd Blackclock bin on to her again?' (Chapter 5). The effect of the convincingly genuine language used is to make us feel we are reading about people, the likes of which might well exist. The impact of the whole novel is thus considerably heightened.

Episodic form

Despite this the novel is much more than simply a description of real life. It has been structured in a calculated manner, crafted carefully to present certain facets of real life. Sillitoe pointed out in his 1970 Introduction that 'it was in progress for seven years before the final typed version was sent to London'. It is an episodic novel and some chapters (such as Chapters 1, 8 and 14) might well stand as short stories on their own. Chapter 14, especially, might be criticized as being an unnecessary digression and yet it serves to develop further Arthur's character whilst at the same time further highlighting the nature of working-class life in Nottingham. Indeed, the abundance of characters produced by this episodic form gives a richness to the novel. Characters such as Mrs Bull, Jane and Jim, Sam, Fred, Bernard Griffin and Uncle George all have an important part to play (even if in Uncle George's case it is the mainly functional role of providing the reason for Arthur not immediately leaving the White Horse – and, therefore, probably avoiding the soldiers). They certainly give the reader the feeling that they are getting to know a whole class of people, and not just one or two individuals. Sillitoe's skill at characterization is such that the minor characters all have their own individuality and do not often fall into stereotypes. Characters such as Fred and Sam are intriguing in their own right; they are obviously complex figures, the surface of whom we barely scratch. In this way, they are like many people we meet in real life: they are obviously interesting, but our acquaintanceship with them is only fleeting.

Narrative technique

We probably know Arthur Seaton better than we know most of our friends and acquaintances in real life. The reason for this is that, though most of the narrative is in the third person *about* Arthur Seaton, we are at times allowed to know what he is actually thinking. For instance, in Chapter 9, when Arthur wonders to himself 'What am I?', we are then allowed into his mind as he attempts to answer the question. The effect of this is that we do get to know Arthur intimately and it is, therefore, likely that we will feel a sympathy for him as we know why he is as he is. Sillitoe's narrative technique in the novel is quite complex, however, as at times we do not see into Arthur's mind but are only told what he does and says. This means we are able to be more objective in our opinions of him as we do not only see the events of the novel from his point of view. He is a character we feel we can understand and sometimes sympathize with and yet we are also able to see the effects of his actions on others and condemn him for them. Our feelings towards Arthur often change, as they do towards people in real life, and like a real person he develops during the novel as he learns from and reacts to the experience of his life. He is the most convincing and rounded character in the novel because we know so much about what he does, says and thinks.

Structure

Other noteworthy elements concerning the structure of the novel include: the flimsiness of the plot and the coincidences contained within it; the neatness of the plot, with all loose ends being tied up; the time-scale of the narrative; the contrasting moods of the novel; and its controlled development towards the climax of Chapter 12, which is then followed by the conclusion of Part 2. The plot is undoubtedly contrived and hinges around such coincidences as Jack and the two soldiers being at the bottom of the Helter Skelter in Chapter 11, Arthur meeting Winnie on the night of Brenda's abortion in Chapter 6 and Doreen being in the White Horse in Chapter 12. All of these occurrences are within the realms of possibility, but all are very convenient and would seem to be included in order to make points about the characters or to bring strands of the story to a neat conclusion. Sillitoe's desire to tie up the loose ends of the novel can be seen in his inclusion of the scene in Chapter 15 where Arthur meets Bill in the pub and they resolve their differences. The time-scale of the novel is slightly confusing. The novel deals with Arthur's development as a character and exact dates are not important. However, at times, there are jumps ahead in time which are not always entirely clear (as between Chapters 3 and 4) and towards the end a whole year seems to go unaccounted for as we are told Arthur is not yet twenty-three in Chapter 11 and yet he tells Doreen he is twenty-four in Chapter 15. As with any criticism of the plot, though, one must ask oneself of what importance this discrepancy is: for the novel reflects reality and does so convincingly, but does not purport to be a factual account of reality.

Changes of mood

One of the novel's strengths is the way in which it is able to convey differing moods, sometimes within the same chapter (as in Chapter 4). This emphasizes the theme of the changeability of life and also makes clear that Arthur's life is by no means a depressing one. It is like most people's lives in the sense that it involves pleasure and responsibility. One of the best examples of the change of mood is when the comic shooting of Mrs Bull in Chapter 8 follows the disturbing Chapters 6 and 7 which deal with the abortion and Arthur's behaviour and thoughts immediately after it. The novel is essentially a serious one and indeed becomes increasingly contemplative in Part II, after the climax of the action has been reached with the savage beating of Arthur in Chapter 12. It is not, though, without humour, especially in

Chapter 8 and, to some extent, in Chapter 14, and it emphasizes throughout that life is to be lived and affords many pleasures.

Language and detail

Above all, the novel's vibrancy and its sense of vitality are conveyed through Sillitoe's precise use of language, his use of imagery and symbolism, and his ability to create atmosphere through the use of telling detail. Examples of these skills abound. One only has to read the opening paragraphs of Chapters 5 and 9 to witness how Sillitoe creates the feel of Nottingham by his choice of individual adjectives and verbs. The overall feeling of the violence of life is strengthened by including details such as Margaret having to stay at her parents' to avoid her husband (Chapter 4), the man hitting the singer for no other reason than that he disliked his singing (Chapter 6), and Jane hitting Jim with the glass (Chapter 14); a detail such as Ralph's first wife having died of consumption points to the harshness of life (especially experienced by the older generation in the novel); and the excessive nature of the young is shown not just by Arthur but by such details as Frank persuading his fiancée to be sick in Chapter 14.

Imagery

As with *Loneliness*, *Saturday* is particularly notable for its use of imagery and symbolism. Sometimes, we are simply confronted by an unexpectedly flamboyant image blazing out of the page at us, creating an exact and vivid picture. Whether it be that a worker's back looks like a 'string of conkers' when he's on piece-work (Chapter 2) or that Arthur, on being run over in Chapter 7, feels 'as if a coal fire had been rammed into the back of his throat', the effect is striking. Some of the images used recur. Events or feelings are often described in terms of battles or fighting: when drunk Arthur has 'battles with lampposts and walls' (Chapter 1); when it arrives the new year swings its fist (Chapter 9); and, in Chapter 15, Arthur realizes that, though he is 'fighting the last stages of an old battle' (in curbing his lifestyle), in his relationship with Doreen, he is 'feeling the first skirmishes of a new conflict'. Arthur himself is described a number of times in terms of wild animals, emphasizing his primitive and rebellious nature: in Chapter 1 we are told of 'the beast inside Arthur's stomach' making its 'appalling growl' as he is sick; in Chapter 7 his 'existence' is described as having fangs and claws and he roars 'like a bull'; and Doreen warns him she will 'tame' him in Chapter 14. Such a small number of examples does not do full justice to the range and originality of Sillitoe's imagery, but does give some idea of how the novel is brought to life by his use of imagery and how certain impressions are thereby implanted in the reader's mind.

Symbolism

Sillitoe also uses symbolism to good effect. This depends on the reader's ability and willingness to interpret events and to look at them in a wider context. If we attempt to do this in *Saturday*, we can see how many otherwise seemingly irrelevant incidents serve to illustrate and emphasize the novel's main themes. The title itself is not without significance: Saturday night can be seen as symbolic of pleasure, enjoyment and even excess, whereas Sunday morning is when any consequences of the previous night have to be faced up to and, moreover, is a time of reflection and contemplation. The whole of Part I shows Arthur unrelentingly seeking indulgent, selfish pleasure; in Part II, he has to come to terms with the consequences of his excessive lifestyle and reflects on the future (once he has recovered from his metaphorical 'hangover' in Chapter 13). Symbolism might also be seen in the way Arthur dresses; his cheating at darts (Chapter 3); his poker-playing (Chapter 5); his rolling of pennies (Chapter 12); and his successful bet on Fairy Glory (Chapter 14).

Selectivity, clarity and the ending

So, the novel does indeed reek of life, and it does so because of the skills of the writer. To create his effects, he has been selective in his choice of subject matter: no chapters are spent on those parts of Arthur's life which lack incident. Consequently, we are carried along by the pace of the novel and the idea of Arthur's life being lived in a whirlpool is successfully created. Most importantly, Sillitoe creates his world clearly (thereby living up to his own belief, expressed in his autobiographical essay, *The Long Piece*, that 'Good English is clear English'). He does not try to impress us with learning or write ambiguously, but writes explicitly and provocatively, and provides us with no easy answers. Arthur is optimistic at the end, but his forthcoming marriage to Doreen certainly does not provide a conventional happy ending. Rather than rounding the novel off, it leaves us wondering as to how Arthur's life will continue to develop.

Revision questions

Test your knowledge of *Saturday Night and Sunday Morning* by answering the following questions.

1 What is the nickname given to the ex-sailor who has a drinking match with Arthur?

2 Where was Arthur riding when knocked down by a lorry?

3 What Sunday newspaper do Brenda and Jack take?

4 At home, with whom does Arthur share a bed?

5 What, according to Arthur, does his father do from six to eleven every night?

6 What is Arthur's job?

7 What is Arthur's usual wage?

8 How many children has Margaret?

9 How old was Arthur when he first started working at the factory?

10 Who is the only named character in the novel that owns a car?

11 What is Mrs Seaton's remedy for Arthur's stomach upsets?

12 What meal does Mrs Seaton prepare as a special pay-day treat?

13 How much does Arthur pay his mother for his board?

14 How does Brenda first attempt to abort the baby?

15 What was the name of Ada's first husband?

16 How did he die?

17 With what record do the Tribe taunt Ralph?

18 At what sort of factory did Brenda and Em'ler work together?

19 What is Arthur's nickname for Winnie?

20 Where is Bill stationed?

21 Why does Fred not help Arthur in the fight caused by the dart?

22 Why does the man throw his beer glass through the undertaker's window?

23 To whom is Mrs Bull talking when she is shot?

24 Whom does she initially think has shot her?

25 In what month does the Goose Fair take place?

26 What is Arthur's father's Christian name?

27 With whom does Arthur go out every night whilst on military training to get drunk?

28 In what pub does Arthur unexpectedly meet Brenda and Winnie?

29 In what pub does Arthur first meet Doreen?

30 In what month is Arthur's birthday?

31 On what day does Arthur take Doreen to the Goose Fair?

32 Which film star does Arthur mention when talking to William, when talking to Doreen and whilst creating havoc on the Ghost Train?

33 Where does Arthur tell Jack he drinks on a Friday night?

34 What does Uncle George do for a living?

35 How long does Arthur remain in a half-sleep after he is beaten up?

36 A bet on which horse wins Arthur £12?

37 Whose friend is Sam's?

38 From what country does Sam originate?

39 Who is aged thirty and has ginger hair?

40 In what pub does Arthur accidentally spill his drink over a woman?

41 To whom is Colin married?

42 Who, at Ada's house at Christmas, wears a pilot officer's uniform?

43 Which of Ada's Tribe is tubercular?

44 What game do Ada's Tribe play after Christmas Dinner?

45 What are the names of Ada's two unmarried sisters?

46 Which member of Arthur's family had been a blacksmith?

47 From what city does Chumley originate?

48 What is the only part of the newspaper Mrs Greatton does not read?

49 When pretending to leave the Greattons' house, why does Arthur shout his farewell to Doreen?

50 Where will Arthur and Doreen live when they marry?

General questions and a sample answer in note form

1 'Arthur Seaton is drunken, ill-behaved and immoral.' Do you think this description sums him up?
Suggested notes for essay answer:

He is:
(a) drunken: Chapters 7 and 14 show him drinking heavily; during his 15 days' military training in Chapter 9 he is drunk every night.
(b) ill-behaved: numerous examples include: vomiting over the middle-aged couple, committing adultery, putting the dead mouse beneath the woman's drill, overturning the car, cheating at darts and poker, shooting Mrs Bull, ruining the couple's enjoyment on the Ghost Train.
(c) immoral: again his adultery, his excessive drinking, his frequent flouting of convention (as in his underage voting), his ready acceptance of abortion, his helping to steal beer from a pub cellar.

And yet by no means does this sum him up. There is much more we need to say about him. He is:
(a) *reckless*, as shown in the indiscreet way he conducts his affair with Brenda
(b) *carefree*, as shown in his behaviour at the Goose Fair on the Saturday night
(c) *violent*, as shown in the fight over the dart
(d) *quick-witted*, as when he sees Jack in the Athletics Club and immediately provides Brenda with her alibi for not being there
(e) *self-centred*, as shown by his reaction to Brenda's being pregnant
(f) *kind*, as shown by his dealings with the children Jacky and William
(g) *deceitful*, as shown in his feigned friendship with Jack
(h) *destructive*, as shown by his overturning the car and when he is on military training
(i) *opportunistic*, as shown by the two occasions we see him meet and sleep with Winnie
(j) *lying*, as shown when he tells his mother he fell off a gasometer

Other adjectives which might be considered when trying to sum up Arthur include: irresponsible, defiant, independent, insensitive, uncaring, rebellious, attractive, cunning, charismatic, dangerous, pleasure-seeking, belligerent, maturing, free, dynamic, self-satisfied, callous, unrepentant, generous, frustrated, cocksure, bored, high-spirited.

Conclusion Like a real person, Arthur is a complex character and cannot be adequately summed up by three words. When assessing him, it is important to remember his age and upbringing: he is only young, has had little moral guidance and has to learn about life through his own experiences. He does things that we must condemn, but, ultimately, he is not a bad person. He is selfish and this is a consistently dislikable trait, but he never seeks to initiate hurt. Despite his faults, we admire much in Arthur: his independence, his resilience, his personal integrity and his increasing self-awareness. It is important that he develops as a character: he is not as selfish at the end of the novel as at the beginning, and he has come to realize that he must curb his lifestyle and that he must consider the needs and feelings of other people. So, the description in the title might sum up his behaviour in Chapter 1, but it does not sum up the more mature, thoughtful and considerate Arthur that we see develop by the last chapter.

2 In what ways do you think that Arthur Seaton is a different person at the end of the novel than he was at the start?

3 Assess the significance of four of the following characters in the novel: Mrs Bull, Sam, Mrs Greatton, Winnie, Fred, Uncle George, Em'ler.

4 Do you feel any sympathy for Jack in the novel? What are his strengths and weaknesses as a husband and as a man?

5 Do you think that Arthur and Doreen are well suited to one another? In what ways do you think their marriage will be successful and what will be its problems?

6 Why do you think there is so much violence in the novel? Are any of the outbursts of violence justifiable? Is violence ever justifiable?

7 Sillitoe describes Arthur as just 'another drop of water' in the 'ocean' of life. Do you think this sums up the place of the individual in society?

8 At the end of the novel, did you feel depressed or optimistic? Why?

9 Assess the role of women in the novel. Which woman do you most admire and why?

10 One phrase used in the novel to describe life is the 'common battleground of the jungle'. In what ways might life in all classes of society be said to be a jungle?

11 Many have praised the novel for its accuracy and realism. In what ways does Sillitoe achieve this?

12 Take one chapter or episode from the novel and say why you think it is particularly significant to the story as a whole.

13 Either (a) write a short story describing Arthur's wedding day, or (b) write a short story involving Arthur in ten years' time.

14 Examine Sillitoe's use of language in the novel and how he succeeds in creating atmosphere. You might consider: the way in which the characters speak; the use of slang; the imagery and symbolism.

15 Near the beginning Arthur declares to himself: 'Don't let the bastards grind you down.' Do you feel he succeeds or fails to live up to this statement?

16 In 1967 a mother protested to her local education authority at the novel being taught in her daughter's school. Would you support her protest or do you feel that there is anything to be gained from studying the novel?

17 Do you feel rebellion is always bound to fail?

18 Write a short story set in the present day which involves a young rebellious person defying authority or the accepted conventions of society.

19 'Luck was always changing.' Either write a short story or relate experiences in your own life which bear out the truth of this sentence from the novel.

20 Write about the pleasures and frustrations of life as shown in *Saturday Night and Sunday Morning*.

The Loneliness of the
Long-Distance Runner

Plot summary

I

Smith, a seventeen-year-old from Nottingham, tells of his long-distance cross-country running whilst at a Borstal in Essex. He is allowed to run alone in the surrounding countryside by the Governor, who hopes Smith will win the national Borstal Blue Ribbon Prize Cup. Smith tells of his thoughts – anti-establishment and alienated – whilst running, even though he feels that 'it's daft to think deep'.

II

Smith explains why he is in Borstal. When his father died of cancer of the throat, his mother received £500 insurance money. Smith enjoys the luxury in which they now live (and, especially, the new television set), but after six weeks of idleness he becomes restless. So one foggy night he wanders around the streets with his 'pal', Mike. They see an open window in a baker's backyard; Smith climbs in and they steal the cashbox. It contains over £150 which they hide up the drainpipe 'outside the door in the back-yard' of Smith's house. Smith, convicted for a similar crime previously, is questioned a number of times by a plain-clothes detective. Finally, the detective calls one morning when it is raining heavily; Smith, out of spite, does not invite the detective into the house. Whilst he stands on the doorstep, the rain washes the money out of the drainpipe. Smith is sent to Borstal; it is Mike's first conviction and he is put on probation.

III

It is the day of the race. The Governor is expectant, the day is 'full of sunshine' and Smith is the favourite to win. He runs smoothly and by half-way takes the lead; he muses about life and does not concentrate on the race. For the first time since it happened, he thinks about his father's death and the horrific moment when he discovered him. As the end of the five-mile race approaches and he comes in sight of the crowd, he has a big lead over a runner from Gunthorpe. He is determined to lose and slows down deliberately, allowing the Gunthorpe man to pass him and win. The disappointment of the Governor marks a moment of triumph for Smith against the establishment. After the race, in his final six months in Borstal, he is punished by being given all the dirtiest jobs. On leaving Borstal, he avoids National Service because he has contracted pleurisy; this pleases him. He continues his thieving and, at the time of writing, he has just stolen £628 and is planning 'an even bigger snatch'. He reveals that he has written the story while idling after his latest theft and part of its purpose is to spite the Governor – though he knows the Governor would not understand it if he read it.

Critical commentary and textual notes

I

to tell you the truth From the beginning we are directly talked to and
confided in; the effect is that we are drawn into the world of the story
and into feeling sympathy for Smith.

very fair lick A very good (fast) speed.

slum-gullion Stew (slang).

nothing but a mug's game A colloquial saying meaning that it would be
a very foolish thing to do. The idea of life as a 'game' is one which
Smith uses frequently throughout the story, even if he himself is not
prepared to abide by the rules.

watching out over the drives . . . from the tops of tanks Smith sees life
as a war between 'us' and 'them'; he equates establishment figures with
the enemy of World War II, the Germans.

if you can believe what I'm trying to say Smith feels alienated from
the whole world and never expects to be believed. Again, the effect is
that we feel more sympathy for him because he is trying to
communicate, to tell his feelings to *us*.

a shimmy A vest.

shagged Exhausted (slang).

kicked the bucket Died. Notice how Smith speaks in colloquial English.

**I have the feeling that it's going to get colder . . . a thousand miles of
ice** The frostiness of the weather as Smith runs (wearing only his
'shimmy and shorts') is symbolic of his relationship with the world: he
finds it a hostile place and has little with which to protect himself.

'If you play ball with us, we'll play ball with you' Sillitoe has the
Governor speak in simple clichés to Smith to emphasize how those in
authority are patronizing to those who are being punished.

we was Grenadier Guards The grammatical error of 'was' instead of
'were' reminds us of Smith's lack of education. The image of
'Grenadier Guards' (a first-rank regiment in the British army)
reinforces the idea of life as a war.

**In-law blokes like you and them, all on the watch for Out-law blokes
like me and us** Smith is very much an Outsider; he realizes that we,
the readers, are probably not like him.

pulling our puddings Masturbating.

It's a treat being a long-distance runner . . . from the next street Smith
does enjoy his running and the aloneness it affords him; after all,
contact with the world has only resulted in trouble and failure.

It's a good life . . . bastard-faced In-laws The story's major theme of defiance of the establishment; cf Arthur Seaton's 'Don't let the bastards grind you down.'

swaddies See note p. 36 of *Saturday*.

almost as he'd talk to his prize racehorse Smith sees himself as being treated merely as a possession, no more than a prized animal. He has no sense of common humanity with establishment figures such as the Governor.

sling my hook Make off, clear out (slang).

I'll have more fun and fire out of my life than he'll ever get out of his Pleasure and excitement are Smith's only goals in life. He has no beliefs, no higher ideals. He seeks only transitory pleasures: he expects no more.

have a whip-hand Having an advantage or control over.

to say that last sentence has needed a few hundred miles of long-distance running It is important to remember that the whole story is a result of Smith's intense thinking. We are reminded that, like everything else in his life, the story has not come easily to him.

don't and never will so help me God Almighty Notice how the writing becomes less grammatical and coherent when Smith gets excited.

It's like me rushing up to thump a man ... to stick me like a pig Smith's mind readily conjures up images of violence and aggression. 'Stick like a pig' means either to kill an animal by thrusting a knife into its throat or, simply, to spear it.

this unarmed combat doesn't amount to much Another war image: one which possibly sums up Smith's life.

dobbie An assault with the fists, a punch-up (slang).

They can drop all the atom bombs they like for all I care Notice Smith's lack of concern with the nuclear threat, the major worry of the time.

at Dartmoor ... at Lincoln It is such prisons which provide the battle-grounds in Smith's war.

nowt Nothing (dialect).

scrumping Stealing.

batting their tabs Clipping their ears (slang).

clambed to death To be extremely hungry.

It's a good job ... I'd have dropped the whole thing weeks ago Note the realism and the sense of pointlessness.

a phlegmy bit of sunlight A startlingly original image, typical of Sillitoe. Typical of Smith is its unpleasant, distorted way of seeing something most people view as beautiful.

like a cut-balled cockerel Another striking image, which emphasizes Smith's pride, but also shows how he feels castrated by his imprisonment and barely in control of his actions.

there I was whizzing down the bank and not seeing a bloody thing Smith, despite his talent for running, or otherwise, thinks life and circumstances (as symbolized by 'them big trees') are always going to trip him up at some time, however well he is doing.

II

Now I believe ... a wad of crisp blue-black fivers ... shopkeeper's till Smith continues to confide his beliefs. Here he tells us of his belief in living for the moment and as expensively as possible, a belief not uncommon in the 1950s as luxury items became increasingly more accessible.

she ordered ... a new carpet because the old one was covered with blood from dad's dying and wouldn't wash out Smith is very matter-of-fact about his father's death: his difficult life has resulted in his being emotionally hardened.

lolly Money (slang).

Night after night ... mam was with some fancy-man upstairs on the new bed she'd ordered This is another instance of the taking of pleasure whenever possible. Smith's own lack of conventional morality might be partly explained by the immoral, pleasure-seeking example he has been set by his mother.

hot-chair Colloquial expression for the electric chair, a means of execution.

we played some good tricks with the telly The television allows the Smith family to enjoy an unaccustomed sense of superiority. For a change Smith is dictating as to what will happen.

It was the best of all though when we did it to some Tory Smith's hatred of the establishment is seen again.

owt Anything (slang).

we didn't know where the housefronts began what with the perishing cold mist all around In the less environment-conscious 1950s such mists were not infrequent. Here the situation is symbolic of the aimlessness, ignorance and purposelessness of Smith and Mike.

Snatched to death Colloquial expression meaning very cold.

peepers Eyes (slang).

ham-hock shoulders A hock is the joint between the knee and fetlock of an animal's hindleg. Here the phrase is used metaphorically to emphasize Mike's muscularity.

Dolly-on-the-Tub Pregnant woman (slang).

I suppose the only reason why I was pals with him was because I didn't say much ... either Smith's introspective nature is shown; he does not find it easy to, nor does he seem particularly to desire to, communicate with other people. He does not seem to have any close friends.

Gatling – Gun A nineteenth century machine-gun with clustered barrels, presumably seen by Smith in Westerns on television.

like they was the adjustable jack-spanner under a car Smith's description of Mike's palms is typical of him: it effectively creates the picture by using a simile taken from everyday working class life.

yaling locks Another example of Smith's creative use of language. Here he has invented a word. A Yale lock is a popular form of lock and this phrase presumably refers to Smith's ability to open or pick such locks.

dirty words like muck and spit Rhyme shows the words he really means. In 1959 it was still illegal to print certain words deemed to be obscene.

I looked at an ever-loving babe . . . so blew it a kiss The intimate way in which Smith refers to the typewriter is in marked contrast to his coldness towards people. This is possibly because he knows that the typewriter is more reliable, in that it is actually worth money, whereas Smith is very wary and suspicious of other people.

narks Police spies (slang).

tripe-twisting pain Colloquial expression meaning extreme pain. Tripe is a word vulgarly used to describe one's entrails.

big batchy head Big stupid head (slang).

if you can call all that thinking It is thinking, but, more than that, this paragraph shows both Smith's imagination and his urge to outwit the establishment, as he does the slow-witted policeman in his fantasy.

sincere, honest, hardworking, conscientious blokes like Mike and me This clearly outlines Smith's warped interpretation of life; most of the story suggests the opposite would provide a more accurate description.

Some people are so mean-gutted . . . Smith views people as aggressively competitive and self-centred; this belief helps to fashion his own behaviour.

skiffle A type of music (involving a band accompanying a singing guitarist or banjoist) popular in the late fifties.

dick Detective (slang).

a snotty yes or no Such a phrase reminds us of the biased nature of the narration; we only have Smith's version of events. It is impossible for us to tell whether the policeman was really 'snotty' (colloquial for short-tempered) or not.

nicky-hat Slang for a hat worn by someone in prison or Borstal, 'nick' being a vulgar word for prison.

jackses Vulgar word, here used metaphorically for hindquarters.

Back in the ring, but this was worse than a boxing match Appropriate image, as life is one long fight for Smith. Later he extends the metaphor as he tells us he is 'winning on points'.

there's a lot of them against only one Smith knows he is doomed to failure because of the power of authority; none the less, he is a genuine rebel and will always continue to battle with authority.

It might come sooner than anybody thinks, like in Hungary In 1956, without prior warning, Russia invaded Hungary; the naturally rebellious Smith hopes a similarly unexpected upheaval might occur in Britain.

get my lawyer on the blower, will you? In his parody of an upper class villain (probably the result of watching detective shows on television), Smith again shows his lively sense of humour.

it's like a game almost For Smith, the game is 'Us against Them.'

Judging by his flash-bulb face The detective's face brightens up immediately: Smith's imaginative mind expresses this effectively in this metaphor.

I didn't tell him anything . . . without batting an eyelid Like Arthur Seaton, Smith has no compunction at all about lying whenever it suits him.

a packet of woods Cigarettes, brand-name 'Woodbines'.

buckshee Gratuitous. Here, specifically, without any foundation in fact.

Al Jolson Celebrated Jewish–American singer (1886–1950) who blacked his face to sing songs like *Sonny Boy*.

sleep-logged To sleep like a log means to sleep soundly. This actual word Smith has made up himself.

tick See note p. 23 of *Saturday*.

tips Filter-tip cigarettes.

this time I'd have the bastards beat Smith is defiant of and determined to beat authority. Unlike the 'lucky' Arthur Seaton, he is destined to lose, at least on this occasion.

hoss-tods Horse turds.

green-backs Pound notes. (There were no pound coins in 1959.)

his hand clamped itself on to my shoulder The section ends symbolically, with the figure of authority unshakeably fastening on to the rebel.

III

lace-curtain lungs, a football heart, and legs like varicose beanstalks Smith is able to produce imaginative imagery to describe a decaying human being. The sense of 'football heart' is unclear, possibly it means blown up to the size of a football through over-exertion.

split my gizzard in spite of my perfect running, and down I fell As at the end of Section I, Smith cannot imagine ultimate success; he feels there will always be someone from authority metaphorically shooting him down. His negative attitude contrasts sharply with that of Arthur

Seaton, who always feels that he will be lucky and will win.

Ivanhoe Originally a novel by Sir Walter Scott (1771–1832). There have been a number of film versions.

a toy rabbit in front and . . . a collier's cosh behind Smith feels that people only do things for two reasons: because they want to gain something for themselves (the whippet wants the toy rabbit) or because they want to avoid punishment (the whippet does not want the collier's cosh). A typically cynical view.

It was hard to understand . . . And the winning post was no end to it Smith's defeatist and depressing beliefs about life, viewed metaphorically in terms of cross-country running. He does not understand it though he knows you have to keep going; he knows it involves dealing with things you know little about and that it contains fear; he knows there are ups and downs, though you do not always realize at the time; he knows there are dangers; and he knows that success ('the winning post') is short-lived.

only time you stopped really . . . stayed dead in the darkness for ever A metaphorical expression of the theme that everything eventually ends in failure. This whole paragraph is important in terms of understanding Smith's character and beliefs.

You should think about nobody . . . bottles of iodine in case you fall Again Smith uses long-distance running as a metaphor for life: here he expresses his belief in independence and not being dictated to by others.

stone-breaking in the way I want to do it and not in the way they tell me Smith is willing to face any punishment meted out – as long as he brings it about. Above all, he is determined not to be dictated to and downtrodden. He wants a personal freedom, even if it is within the bounds of imprisonment.

I only want a bit of my own back . . . before my time is up The story is one of revenge: Smith wants to gain revenge against authority, in however small a way, even though he realizes authority will in turn, and in a bigger way, gain its revenge on him.

And so I'll hit him . . . I planned it longer Smith knows he cannot win the war against authority; none the less, he looks forward to the short-lived pleasure of a surprise victory in this particular 'battle'.

And all this is another uppercut I'm getting in first Notice again the boxing image; Smith realizes he is very much a lightweight matched against a heavyweight. Consequently, any success at all has to be gained by speed or cunning.

threatened to punch her tab Threatened to punch her in the face (slang).

I might just as well win this bleeding race, which I'm not going to do Notice the change of tense employed by Sillitoe here in order to create a greater sense of immediacy – the whole story is written as a recollection, yet here he uses the future tense ('might' and 'going to'). The effect is of Smith reliving the moment and we relive it with him.

our half-dead gangrened gaffer is hollow like an empty petrol drum Again, the extent to which he despises the Governor is reflected in the vehemence and entirely condemnatory nature of the imagery used.

on the floor must have been all the blood he'd had . . . thin and pink It is such memories and experiences as his father's death that have fuelled Smith's anti-authoritarianism, his anger and his hatred. He has been scarred by his background, the unfairness of it, the immorality of his mother and the horror of his father's death.

I hate to have to say this but something bloody-well made me cry Smith rarely shows sensitivity; that he cries here points to the importance (to him) of the gesture that he is making.

By God I'll stick this out . . . I've got guts for this Smith's character is marked by a determination, an immovable stubbornness, as he makes his desperate bid to kick back at society.

Until then I'm a long-distance runner . . . no matter how bad it feels A metaphor which encapsulates Smith's singular, isolated attitude to life. He will be his own man, however much pain it causes him.

blubbing now out of gladness that I'd got them beat Smith's moment of triumph: a rare moment in his life.

don't think I'm not still running, because I am, one way or another Smith, one suspects, will always be running; certainly, his life will never be easy.

one or two books I've read . . . didn't teach me a thing Smith is an unusual fictional figure – he doesn't come out on top, nor does he develop, change or reform. He remains a working class petty thief and one suspects he will always remain so.

Smith

I'm a long-distance runner, crossing country all on my own no matter how bad it feels

In the character of the seventeen-year-old Smith, Alan Sillitoe has created a lasting symbol of discontented youth. The whole story is narrated by Smith and in it he reveals his innermost thoughts; despite the fact that he confesses to being an inveterate liar, we have little doubt that he is telling us the truth about his life. And yet he remains a difficult person to understand. He is aggressive and unprincipled, he has few positive interests in life, he is a thief who finds more pleasure in inanimate objects than other human beings, he speaks in a vulgar and crude manner, he is consistently negative and absolutely irreconcilable with conventional society; despite all this (and partly because it is he who tells the story and we are affected by his confiding in us), he is not unlikeable and it is difficult not to feel sympathy for him. The main reason for this is that we realize he is not a freak to be dismissed or, as by the Governor, patronized, but that he is an individual, a fellow human being. Indeed, his independence is to be admired. He will not bow to pressure. He is doggedly determined to retain his own personality, his own beliefs and, consequently, his self-respect. He knows life will be difficult – he metaphorically sees his whole life being spent stone-breaking – but he is determined it will be difficult on his own terms: it will be 'stone-breaking in the way I want to do it and not in the way they tell me'.

Above all, Smith is an outsider, a problem outsider. He might, traditionally, be viewed as 'a low-down rotten cad' who will not toe the line or, alternatively, he might be seen as an anti-hero, standing up for himself and refusing to be oppressed. He fits neither classification smoothly. He is certainly defiant of authority and rebellious, much more so than the likes of Arthur Seaton. Whether it is by turning down the sound on the television whenever a Tory speaks or whether it is by deliberately losing the race, he takes every opportunity he can to get one over on authority. As he says about losing the race, 'I only want a bit of my own back on the In-laws and Potbellies', and then he cries with pleasure 'that I'd got them beat at last'. Indeed he is not merely defiant of authority: he despises authority. He sees his battle with authority as a war: he might lose, but he will enjoy winning the occasional battle and whenever he can he will 'hit him [any representative of authority] where it hurts a lot'. The extent of his hatred for authority is shown in his reason for leaving the private detective on the doorstep in the pouring rain: 'I wanted him to get double pneumonia and die.'

There is much about Smith which is unattractive. He is scornful and surly. He is a petty thief who glories in the money he steals. He is a self-confessed liar ('I can go on doing that forever without batting an eyelid') and believes that to have principles is 'barmy'. He is often idle ('Night after night we sat in front of the telly'), usually purposeless ('I didn't think about anything at all, as usual'), and completely self-centred ('They can drop all the atom bombs they like for all I care'). And yet he is not like this without reason. Nothing has been easy in his life: even telling his story does not come readily to him, as he struggles to write down his thoughts with his stub of a pencil. And he confesses that the thoughts themselves have taken hundreds of miles of long-distance running to formulate. His lack of natural talent has not been counter-balanced by a privileged or loving upbringing. Smith's mother's main interest in the story is her own sexual pleasure with her string of 'fancy-men'; it seems, even when her husband was alive, she was openly unfaithful. It is her husband's death that has most emotionally scarred Smith. Though he never admits it, he has been deeply affected by his father's death, as shown by the number of references he makes to the horrific scene when he discovered the body: 'on the floor must have been all the blood he'd had in his body, right from the toe-nails up.'

With such a background, lacking moral guidance and containing domestic tragedy, it becomes more difficult simply to condemn Smith. His love of materialistic luxuries and his extravagance become more understandable and, at the same time, are rather sad. On leaving the baker's he is tempted to take the 'ever-loving babe of a brand-new typewriter'; it is significant that he never speaks of another human being in such fond terms. His is a life without love, and he seeks to compensate by stealing and spending extravagantly: 'a wad of crisp blue-black fivers ain't a sight of good . . . unless they're flying out of your hand into some shopkeeper's till'. He has become a loner: he is only pals with Mike because they are both introverted, and neither speaks very much. He shuns any kind of emotion and is deeply embarrassed that he began to cry at the end of the cross-country race. His self-esteem is very low and he is touchingly self-deprecating: he is sure his story is 'boring', refers to himself as 'silly bastard me' and claims: 'I ain't got no more brains than a gnat.'

Despite his problems of upbringing and personality, he refuses to be downtrodden. At no stage is he self-pitying, and he is determined to make the most of his life. 'It's a good life', he declares and he knows his life will be full of 'fun and fire'. He is prepared to suffer for it, but he is determined to experience excitement and pleasure. Smith is a proud young man and he does, in fact, have a lively if undisciplined mind. His thoughts show him to be imaginative and there are even unexpected flashes of humour, such as his comical recounting of Mike's violent streak.

In Smith, Alan Sillitoe has, above all, succeeded in creating a believable character. He is riddled with faults and yet is not without saving graces. He expects failure in life (as when his picture of running and beating the world is ruined by an unexpected bullet which shoots him down), but will not be beaten by it. His character might be ill-directed, but it is also vibrant and irrepressible. And, ultimately and most importantly, it does seem that there is so much more beneath the surface waiting to be discovered and developed. We see this most in the profundity of his thoughts whilst running and in the obvious emotional fulfilment he derives from running. In *Loneliness*, Smith is running in the wrong direction; one ends the story hoping that one day he will be pointed in the right direction – and that then he will begin to win races, and be happy to do so. At the same time, in keeping with what is an unremittingly realistic story, one feels that sadly this is unlikely ever to happen.

Themes

It was hard to understand, and all I knew was that you had to run, run, run, without knowing why you were running . . . and the winning post was no end to it . . .

The problems of life

One of the story's major themes concerns the unfairness of life, the difficulties posed by life, the inexplicability of life and the fact that these problems are never-ending. The problems are that much greater for someone like Smith: poor, under-privileged and often on the wrong side of the law. For such a person, ultimate failure seems inevitable. Smith declares that he is 'always tripped up sooner or later' and believes that the always-running race of life is only stopped 'when you tripped over a tree trunk and broke your neck'. Through the character of Smith, Alan Sillitoe emphasizes the harshness of life and points out the short-lived nature of pleasure; even Smith's dreams end in disappointment: when imagining he is 'beating everybody in the world', suddenly 'bullets split my gizzard in spite of my perfect running, and down I fell'.

Independence and personal integrity

However, the story is not entirely pessimistic: it shows that these difficulties must not be given in to. Life does afford pleasures, and one of those pleasures is to assert your own independence and stick up for yourself: 'It's a good life . . . if you don't give in to the coppers and Borstal-bosses and the rest of them bastard-faced In-laws.' The whole story can be read as being in praise of independence and the right of the individual to freedom of choice. We might think that Smith gains little by deliberately throwing the race and spiting the Governor. He has, though, asserted his own independence by doing so and has shown a determination not to be dictated to by others. By his own code of behaviour, he has retained his integrity (the 'honesty' to which he refers) and, in Smith, the individual is seen to have beaten the pressures of a society to which he feels no obligation.

The title itself points to the importance of retaining one's individuality. It is when running that Smith is able to think clearly and to formulate his opinions on life. He realizes the importance of standing up for what you believe in, as illustrated to him by his father's refusal to go to hospital: 'By God I'll stick this out like my dad stuck out his pain.' The story does not condone Smith's beliefs or behaviour, but it does applaud his right to make his own decisions.

Revenge

To some extent, *Loneliness* also deals with the theme of revenge. Smith might be seen as seeking revenge on society for the death of his father. He does not see the need to follow the rules of a society because of which he has so frequently experienced unfairness. Consequently, he might be viewed as a boy rebel taking revenge on the people who would squeeze him into unwanted conformity.

Other themes

A number of other themes emerge from the story. The importance of background and upbringing in forming a person's character can be clearly seen: Smith might be viewed as an almost inevitable product of an upbringing so lacking in conventional morality and principles. The increasing importance of material goods and owning possessions (honestly or otherwise) is highlighted, both in Smith's stealing and in television advertisements where Smith watches 'some pasty-faced tart going head over heels to get her nail-polished grabbers on to them ["things in shops"].' The selfishness of society, the 'look after no. 1' and 'I'm all right, Jack' beliefs increasingly prevalent in the fifties are shown, both in Smith ('You should think about nobody and go your own way') and the people who are so 'mean-gutted' as to go to any lengths 'just to keep their tuppence out of your reach'. It is a thin line between being independent and selfish; it is a line which Smith frequently crosses. Another theme to emerge is that people tend to do things for only two reasons, gain or fear, like the greyhound which wants to catch the toy rabbit but also wants to avoid the collier's cosh. Further, the story is an indictment of the insensitivity and ineffectuality of Borstals and similar institutions. It is no wonder that Smith does not reform, when he is under the control of such a self-motivated, self-concerned and limited man as the Governor. Alan Sillitoe later wrote to *The Times* that he thought Approved Homes 'an unjust and barbaric form of imprisonment for a child'; *Loneliness* shows this to be the case.

'Us' and 'them'

Possibly the story's most important theme is that of 'Us' and 'Them' as shown by Smith's total discontent with and alienation from authority. Smith is wary and suspicious, aware of 'In-law blokes like you and them, all on the watch for out-law blokes like me and us' and his hatred of the Establishment is such that he declares: 'this is war'. Smith epitomizes the rebelliousness of the late fifties youth; he is a difficult member of society and he does little, if anything, to reconcile himself to society. However, the story highlights how totally inadequate society is in dealing with the likes of Smith. He is patronized or oppressed; he is not talked to as an individual and he is certainly not understood. Alan Sillitoe provides no answer to the situation, but his story condemns the insensitivity and shallowness of the Establishment far more than it does the petty criminality of Smith. Indeed, one ends up sympathizing with Smith and realizing how important it is to maintain one's own individuality, even if a consequence of doing so is suffering. It is easy to understand the importance of running to Smith: 'It's a treat being a long-distance runner, out in the world by yourself with not a soul to . . . tell you what to do.'

Style

Naturalism

As with *Saturday Night, Loneliness* is naturalistic; it is not difficult
to feel that Smith is a 'real' person. This is achieved in a number
of ways. The fact that Alan Sillitoe was himself born and bred in
Nottingham is, of course, an important factor. In the story he
writes of a world he knows well; as the *New Statesman* review of
1959 said: it is the 'study of a section of society which has to be
known at first-hand to be understood. All the imaginative sympathy in the world can't fake this kind of thing.' It is firmly set in
the real Nottingham, and the *Nottingham Guardian Journal*
review mentioned the 'many local references and ... the
allusions to city haunts and institutions'. The naturalistic feel is
heightened by Smith's frame of references as he tells his story:
he talks of everyday, humdrum items; he refers to nothing
unlikely or exotic. Baker's shops appear in every town; many
people spend 'Night after night ... in front of the telly'; and
images such as, 'like they was the adjustable jack-spanner under
a car' are easily understandable and of the everyday world. And,
as so often in the real world, a happy ending does not come
about. Smith himself criticizes the one or two books he has read
'because all of them ended on a winning post' and so he could
not believe in them. We have no problem in believing in *his*
story.

Language

The language Sillitoe employs heightens the feeling that we are
reading a slice of real life. The *Nottingham Evening Post* praised
the 'genuine Nottingham dialect' used in the story. Colloquialisms and clichés, so regularly used in real life, abound.
Smith runs at a 'very fair lick', he wears a 'shimmy' and, at the
end of his run, is 'shagged'. At various times he is 'clambed' and
'snatched to death'; he talks of 'peepers', 'lolly' and 'narks'.
Clichés include Smith's belief that life is 'nothing but a mug's
game' and the Governor's patronizing advice to him: 'If you play
ball with us, we'll play ball with you.' Smith's casual use of

sentence structure and punctuation and his grammatical lapses ('me and Mike') add to the feeling that we are listening to the story of a real person.

First-person narrative

Smith, of course, is not a real person. He is a figment of Sillitoe's imagination, created to facilitate the telling of this particular story. The effect of Sillitoe adopting a persona in this way is not simply to make the story that much more believable. It does allow an appropriately easy free-flowing way of writing; it also creates an immediacy and a sympathy that would be more difficult to achieve with a third person narrator. We sympathize with Smith because he openly confides in us; in the first paragraph he tells us he is going to tell us the truth. Throughout, he addresses the reader directly, even to the extent of questioning whether we can in fact believe what he is 'trying to say'. Through such means, Alan Sillitoe achieves a sense of intimacy: we feel for Smith because, despite his self-confessed problems of communication, he tells his story to us. The reader feels as if he is hearing a confession and has to remind himself that he is hearing a biased report (is the policeman really a 'dirty bullying jumped-up bastard'?) and must remain objective in his judgement. This is not always easy as, by adopting a persona, Sillitoe allows the story to be subjective and emotional. *Loneliness* is intense, aggressive and angry for the very simple reason that so is its teller. Whether or not in real life Smith would be able to communicate so lucidly and vividly is another matter. Often we have the feeling that Sillitoe has granted Smith powers of communication that he would be unlikely to have in real life in order to render the telling of his story that much more effective.

Imagery

One major way in which Sillitoe has done this is through his use of imagery. Throughout, he uses the extended metaphor of cross-country running resembling life. Both are long and arduous, and difficult and unpredictable, and, as winning a race is only a transitory success, so in life pleasures tend to be short-lived. The metaphor also suggests that it is in moments of loneliness, such as to be found in cross-country running, when we are not influenced by others, that we can best analyse our own characters and formulate our own beliefs about life. And cross-country running, like life, provides many trees to trip you up when you think everything is going well.

Images of games and war

The story highlights the competitive nature of life, the striving to beat others, and Sillitoe emphasizes this by using many images to do with games. At one point, Smith actually says life is 'like a game', though he also points out it is a 'mug's game'. He talks of life being a boxing match and elsewhere sees himself as holding a trump card. The aggressive nature of the game of life is clearly pointed to by the abundance of images involving war and violence. Smith imagines bullets splitting his 'gizzard', he talks of the guards 'watching over the fields like German generals from the tops of tanks', he intends to hit people in authority 'where it hurts a lot', he sees life as 'unarmed combat', he describes the plain-clothes detective as 'old Hitler-face' and finally declares: 'this is war'. Such images effectively help to create the sense of hostility and antagonism so prevalent in the story.

Unpleasant and animal images

Sillitoe uses a number of other images to create atmosphere. Smith compares himself a number of times with animals, possibly suggesting his lack of self-regard, his lowly status or his lack of refinement. He sees himself as 'a cut-balled cockerel', as a whippet, as having 'no more brains than a gnat', as being treated as a prize racehorse and he tells us he clutches the pencil with which he writes in his 'paws'. Many images in the story conjure up unpleasant pictures, not surprisingly in the story of a boy so much at odds with life, and even the sun, normally viewed as spreading warmth and happiness, is described as 'phlegmy'. Indeed, the sun shines but rarely in this story where warmth is lacking in so many ways. Smith is often cold and feels that it will get colder and colder until everything is 'covered with a thousand miles of ice'. This might be viewed as symbolic of his personal coldness towards society, and vice versa.

Humour, optimism and the ending

Despite the overall bleakness of the story and the aggression of its imagery, it is not totally depressing. This is partly because of the humour employed and partly because of Smith's irrepressibility. We see humour in Smith's turn of phrase, his sense of imagination and his sense of the absurd, and in his satirical characterization of the patronizing Governor and the other Potbellies.

The second section is the lightest in tone. We smile at Smith's antics while watching the television and his opinions of the programmes; at Mike not knowing it was foggy because of the poor quality of his glasses; at Mike beating up a 'cock-eyed' newcomer to the street because he thought he was staring at him strangely; at Smith's teasing of the detective; and, of course, at the money appearing in front of the detective's eyes at the very same time that Smith is again glibly denying the robbery. And though the story is about a thief with little faith in life, we finish the story celebrating his latest theft, delighted by his continuing buoyancy. Smith never gives up, even in the face of defeat and, though at the end we feel sure he will be caught again and imprisoned (and rightly so), Sillitoe has avoided a feeling of unqualified depression in the reader by finishing at a point of triumph for Smith.

In a story in which Smith frequently confesses that he does not understand life, it is heartening that he finishes with the words, 'That I do know' – maybe there are grounds here for reserved optimism in the reader. It is certainly a sign of Sillitoe's skills that we *want* to feel optimistic for Smith; Sillitoe's narrative technique, his use of language and the way in which he has created his main character ensure that we sympathize with Smith; we are forced to question our superficial judgement of real-life criminals: are they to be condemned out of hand? That we ask ourselves this question is a testament to Sillitoe: he has chosen an unusual subject matter and approached it from an unusual angle – and, in doing so, he has demanded that the reader examines his own sense of perspective. In short, Sillitoe's style of writing in *Loneliness* is original, challenging, vibrant and thought-provoking.

General questions and a sample answer in note form

1 How effective is the language used in the story?
Suggested notes for essay answer:

Though the language is realistic, it is carefully chosen by Alan Sillitoe, and there are three main devices by which he creates his effects: the first-person narrator; imagery; and symbolism.

1 *First-person narrator*
  (a) Confiding: Sillitoe has Smith talk directly to the reader (for example: 'if you can believe what I'm trying to say') and this is effective in that it creates a bond between Smith and the reader. We sympathize with him because he confides in us; we feel sorry for him because he tells his problems to us (for example, he tells us he is only friends with Mike because both of them are so quiet and have no other friends).
  (b) Colloquialisms: abound throughout. These create a sense of realism. The language Smith uses is believable and, therefore, the story is made believable. He talks of 'slum-gullion', 'dobbie' and 'Dolly-on-the-Tub', and he uses phrases such as 'pulling our puddings' and 'batting their tabs'.
  (c) Clichés: similarly real people tend to use clichés to express themselves and so we find in the story. The two-dimensional Governor is especially prone to speak in clichés and thereby we realize what a superficial character he is.
  (d) Grammar: the story contains frequent grammatical inaccuracies. This is effective as it is appropriate to the poorly educated Smith. Though imaginative, his expression is often slack: 'we was Grenadier Guards'.
  (e) Frames of reference: Sillitoe has heightened the realism of the story by referring to actual places in Nottingham (such as Alfreton Road and Papplewick Street). Throughout Smith's character is conveyed by his frames of reference: his idea of an exotic holiday is to go to Skegness or Cleethorpes; he spends most of his time at home 'in front of the telly': and the only allusions he

makes to anything outside his own humdrum world (such as to Ivanhoe or the Second World War) are based on films he has seen.

2 *Imagery* Sillitoe never uses images which go beyond Smith's frames of reference, but does show Smith's imagination and creativity through the images he uses. The imagery used is also effective in emphasizing some of the story's major themes.

(a) war images: Smith dreams of bullets splitting his 'gizzard': sees the policeman as like Hitler; and views life as 'unarmed combat'. All such images illustrate how life is a constant fight for Smith against authority, and how he views the world as a hostile place.

(b) images of games: point to Smith's constant efforts to try to beat the establishment. He sees life as a boxing match, and sees his gesture of losing the race as 'another uppercut I'm getting in first'.

(c) animal images: Smith often describes himself in terms of animals, both illustrating his unrefined nature and the way society often treats him as inferior. He feels the Governor treats him like a 'prize racehorse' and his immense sense of frustration is vividly shown when he describes himself as a 'cut-balled cockerel'.

(d) unpleasant images: Smith often describes things in an unusually unpleasant manner, suggesting his disillusionment with life. Even the sun he sees as 'phlegmy'.

(e) other images: sometimes the language is effective simply because of the strikingly original and yet accurate nature of the imagery, as when we are told of the 'flash-bulb face' of the detective when he thinks he has caught Smith out or when the Governor is so appropriately described as 'like an empty petrol drum'.

3 *Symbolism* The language used is often effective in suggesting more to the reader than it actually says. Such incidents as the detective's hand *clamping* down on Smith's shoulder (suggesting that, despite his efforts, he is unable to escape the powerful grip of authority) and Smith's tripping up when in full flight (suggesting that however well one is doing life is always likely to present one with unexpected problems) represent more to the reader than simple incidents.

Conclusion The language is effective because it is so appropriate to the type of story being told. It has the ring of truth about it and yet, despite its simplicity, the language is thought-provoking and illustrates Smith's character and the story's themes. Never do we feel the language used by Sillitoe would be beyond Smith, and yet it suggests ideas to the reader which Smith himself would find difficult to express.

2 Do you find Smith a sympathetic or unsympathetic character? Give reasons for your answer.

3 'I'll have more fun and fire out of my life than he'll ever get out of his' (Smith of the Governor). Assess Smith's beliefs about life and comment on what you feel are their shortcomings.

4 Is Smith an insoluble problem? Do you feel it would be possible to integrate him more successfully into society and, if so, how?

5 Write a further episode in the life of Smith. You might write in the first person as Smith, or you might write a third-person story about Smith.

6 Assess the importance of the other characters in the story. What is the importance of their rôles and to what extent do they influence the character of Smith? You should consider Smith's parents, Mike, the Governor and the plain-clothes detective.

7 Write a short story in which the main character is ill at ease with society.

8 What do you think are the advantages and disadvantages of imprisoning criminals? What do you think should be the aims of the penal system and how should these aims be successfully carried out?

Comparative questions on *Saturday Night and Sunday Morning* and *Loneliness of the Long-Distance Runner*

1 What are the similarities and differences between the characters of Arthur and Smith?

2 What similarities do you find in Sillitoe's use of language in the two texts?

3 Examine Sillitoe's use of humour in the two texts.

4 What themes are common to both texts?

5 Write a short scene from a play in which Arthur and Smith meet in a Nottingham pub.

6 To what extent should a person be able to do whatever he wants in a democratic society?

7 Both Arthur and Smith are hardened liars. Do they benefit or suffer from their lying? In your conclusion, give your opinions as to whether you think lying can ever be condoned.

8 What do you feel you have learned about life from reading the two texts?

A Sillitoe Selection
Introduction

This choice of eight stories shows Sillitoe at his best. As so often, he is here largely concerned with childhood, the only exceptions being 'The Fishing-Boat Picture' and 'Uncle Ernest'. Certain themes common to his writing occur: the theme of loneliness, of escape from authority, or poverty, or both (deprivation leads to stealing, petty crime and, in one instance, to suicide), the need for pleasure, excitement. The sense of realism gives them an immediate authenticity. Throughout there runs the natural idiom of the people with their unforced freedom of expression. You will find the stories moving and sometimes funny, regardless of your own background and the changed times in which we live. Look carefully at the introduction to these stories, the notes and questions which follow them, and the photographs which capture the Nottingham scene. Above all, consider what the author tells us about himself and his writing, since this is important to a full appreciation of the stories and his craftsmanship in them.

The brief commentaries which follow here are a supplement to the stories and the suggestions in the book: the aim is to make you think about what you read and guide you to an appreciation of the material.

The Bike

This story is told in the first person by a fifteen-year-old. Note at once the naturalness of the working-class family scene, the inter-action between the brothers, the economic necessity for the narrator to go to work, and the ease and fluency of the dialogue with the authentic dialect and local references built in (wok, pit-prop, nowt, tab). Colin recalls an incident from his past, one that took place in the school garden. This anticipates his being taken advantage of later by Bernard. Colin's language is vivid, his imagination active, as we see from the Russian reference and the passing violence in the gap idea, as well as the images of the boxing-glove and the hot wallet. The story shows Colin's trusting nature. It also gives us an insight into the pleasures of the time, in Bernard's case the radiogram and the jazz records, in Colin's the idea of speed. There is also the irony that he has *thought* of stealing a bike; he is later to find himself in possession of a stolen one, a kind of poetic justice for his having had such thoughts. Colin dreams of freedom on the bike, a comment on his mono-tonous way of life and equally monotonous way of work; the image of the giant's scarf reflects his need. We register his father's sympathy for what he wants to do when he lends him the money, and the wonderful way his imagination takes off. It promises freedom from the prison of monotony – 'like sawing through the bars in clink' – but also it shows the urban boy's appraisal of reality, 'where fresh air smelt like cowshit'. The climax to the story is well done. The language of the exchanges and the attitude of onlookers, Colin's knowledge that he has been 'conned', the reflex resort to lying (and quite a convincing lie at that), all this shows Sillitoe's art. Note the contrast between the humour evident in the dialogue and the pathos of the story as the boy's major outlet for happiness disappears. And notice how in his bitterness Colin reverts to the idea of the revolution. The time, the place, the frustrations, the inheritance of petty crime, the poverty trap are all there, and references to Malcolm Campbell (the racing driver who broke land, speed and water records) and to having a DA (Duck's Arse) haircut give the genuine period flavour.

The Ragman's Daughter

From the humorous opening onwards this is a gripping story. The narrator looks back over his stealing career, which began with his self-education – you have to cheat to win – at infants' school. Interestingly, although he becomes a compulsive thief, he admits that once he has taken something he loses interest in it. A lot of stuff he dumps or gives away anonymously; there is a kind of Robin Hood bravado about his activities. The tone is personal, relaxed, colloquial, almost confiding. These reminiscences lead back inevitably to his affair with Doris, although he admits at the outset that he preferred stealing to girls.

Tony, the narrator, tells Doris the truth about where he gets his money from. They come to an agreement – he to steal for money, she for 'kicks', that is, the sheer delight of it. Note, as always, the vividness of the language (for example, of the girl's father: 'a deadbeat skinflint with a pound note sign between his eyes and breathing LSD all over the place'). Their walks, their clinches, are graphically described, and we feel that Doris, scrap-dealer's daughter and grammar-school girl, is going with Tony for kicks too. Their first robbery yields her the money, and Tony indulges his native eccentricity by sticking stamps on the corners that they pass. It is almost as if he enjoys the dare, the idea of nearly, but not quite, leaving a trail.

The thieving, kicks and romance are blended, particularly when Doris comes to visit Tony on her horse. Again the language is vividly descriptive – the horse is 'the colour of best bitter', a comparison drawn from eighteen-year-old Tony's habitual observation. The horse (called Marian, appropriately endorsing the Robin Hood suggestions) leads Tony into romantic contemplation; he sees himself and Doris as playing roles similar to those in the films that they would be used to seeing. In fact Tony is incurably romantic in his daydreams, and these too are an escape from sordid reality. Yet their naturalness together is emphasized, their sexual coming together beautifully defined in 'Not having to chase and fight for it made it seem like real love.' Their sexual mutuality is almost innocent in its intensity, and not without elements of humour – 'we'd have it over and over so that my legs wobbled as I walked back down the stairs.'

The Robin Hood element is seen again in their putting loot through letter boxes and in bins for tramps to pick up. There is a high-spirited adventurousness about this, though we feel the sense of tension, the risks, the inevitability of being caught. With the acquisition of the motor-bike they take trips into the countryside (note the typical industrial landscape, with slag-heaps among the fields). The final job is fraught with irony, since Doris really does not want to do anything that evening – or is it that she has an intuition that something will go wrong? The atmosphere of tension is maintained through the darkness, and broken by Doris deciding to do things for 'kicks' by switching the light on. There follows the almost unbearable delay, and the continuing tension as she tries on the shoes. The sense of dare which characterizes the story is here carried to the extreme which makes for disaster. The awareness which Tony shows by switching off the light precipitates the chase, the panic, the delusory escape. Intuitively, Tony knows that it is the end: typically, he drops the fifty pounds into the letter box. The tale comes to a close with the arrival of the policemen and the three-year stint in Borstal.

By the end of the story – despite the vigour and humour in the telling – we realize that Tony has looked back in anguish, for he has lost both his freedom and Doris. This realization is compounded by the facts of Doris's marriage, her death, and the existence of the baby who is named after him. It is his anguish, one feels, which causes him to steal for the last time. Tony works out his salvation through physical activity. In a sense, seeing the old man with his (Tony's) son makes the story something like the films Tony used to watch. Tony has come through the darkness (he calls Borstal 'three years in the dark') and into the light of solid working existence. The ending is interestingly ambiguous, or at least powerfully suggestive of two things: tragedy brings you to your senses and you survive by graft, by getting on with life. On the other hand, you have the 'haunting' of the 'waking dreams'. Not surprisingly, for Tony the dream is of Doris riding the horse down the street. Despite the terrible reality, he has retained the romance. There is no overt moral to the story – we take the narrative as a slice of life at a particular period in youth. It is sad, in parts cynical, but it is moving and poignant because it captures rebellion, rejection and the assertion of independence. It also stresses the fleeting nature of happiness.

Noah's Ark

This story conjures up the excitement of the fairground, something it shares with a memorable sequence in *Saturday Night and Sunday Morning*. The first emphasis is on poverty and deprivation, seen in ten-year-old Colin's rags and his nickname. Colin is led by Bert but he has a conscience, thinking of what he could buy for fourpence in the way of food or cigarettes for his parents. He gets some cigarettes by scrounging from packets on their way to the fair; the boys' childish unawareness of sexuality is stressed, the atmosphere of excitement is everything. Bert's stealing is discovered but he gets away with it, aided and abetted by Colin. The spending spree with its modest gain is soon over, and the dangerous searching for pennies beneath the Noah's Ark is begun, soon abandoned for begging. The crowded atmosphere, the edge of violence, the courting of danger continues, leading to the tense moment when Colin rides on the Noah's Ark, having been rehearsed by Bert in what he must do in order to avoid paying. Such is Colin's fascination for the ride that he stays on a second time, thus facing detection head on. The tension and danger are vividly conveyed by the style, which reflects the speed and Colin's fear. When the attendant turns and spots him – note the powerful image of the chicken with its wrung neck – Colin's fear is skilfully evoked by the confusion of his thoughts with the movement of the roundabout and the unbearable crescendo of sounds. The climax is Colin's jump from the speeded-up roundabout, the reaction of their both staying out late knowing that they are going to get 'pasted' when they get home, and the final bravado of singing the songs (you should note what they are about) to keep up their spirits.

The presentation of the two boys is realistic and compassionate. Colin is imaginative and intelligent, a boy who reads much but has to come to terms with the hard world in which he finds himself. Bert is an opportunist intent on survival by thieving and conning, but note his loyalty to Colin and his carrying him until 'both donkey and burden crashed out of sight by the bottom roundabout boards where no one went'. This is very sad; both boys are children who lack the freedom and security of childhood.

The Fire-Bug

Again we have the technique of the first-person narrator looking back from the vantage point of maturity. His supposed self-record is of a withdrawn child, but the 'still waters run deep' appraisal of his aunt is the first inkling of his obsession. The initial reaction of the little boy to the fire engine is overwhelming, and the atmosphere of childhood – being slung out, going to the pictures, drawing patterns in the tar – is, as always with Sillitoe, finely conveyed. The development of the obsession is traced unerringly, with insight too into the working of the boy's imagination, the bells he *thinks* he hears. From the start it is a love-fear compulsion; note the Great Fire of London and lying in bed wondering if the house will burn down. Note too the evocative descriptions ('fires were lit like cherry trees', for example), and how these contribute to the sense of excitement and compulsion. After the Bonfire Night blaze there is another section where the narrator looks back: the little fires with the matches, the dislike of getting wet – rain 'seemed to stick into me like falling penknives' – and, above all, the incident with the grown-up cousin.

After he is punished he develops another fear – that of being sent to Cumberland Hall – and this motivates the boy to go far away for his next fire; he goes to the woods, where there is less chance of being caught and the prospect too of making a bigger fire. The caning is followed by a short account of the futility of war expressed with the unsophisticated sincerity of the child. The Sunday expedition is a mixture of bravado – he has matches and paper sticking out of his pockets – and naturalness, like the little rebellion of peeing in the canal. The journey and the entry into the wood are full of expectation and observation, little gems of description, down to the anticipation of the trees sweating when the fire gets going. The vivid language approximates to the boy's feelings – the fire 'went chewing its way up into the air like a shark in Technicolor'. But there is also the pathos of taking to the wood 'like a kid to hot dinners'.

The 'ragged-arsed thunderbolt' tastes of anti-climax; the boy feels a sadness he doesn't understand at what he has done. Then, as he turns towards home, he hears the fire-engines, remembers a factual fire in Mitchell Street, sees the real fire engines, and feels faint as he did all those years ago when he first heard and saw one. Now his triumph, and his fear, concentrate on the six fire engines which will try to put out his fire. The irony is in the last section of the story – the burning of Snakey Wood, the building of the housing estate and, perhaps most important of all, the recovery of the boy's mother. He lit fires when she didn't want him or was ill; now, his security restored, his obsession disappears. But the power of that obsession and its dangers, and the deprivations that lead to that kind of escapist behaviour, have been sensitively and movingly charted by the author.

On Saturday Afternoon

This story, again told in the first person, is a mixture of pathos, tragedy and humour. There is the irony of the time – Saturday afternoon being for relaxation and entertainment – and the self-indulgence of the narrator, who is witnessing something better than the 'pictures' of which he is deprived. But first there is a graphic account of the domestic mood which is generated by poverty and frustration, and this prepares us for the attempted suicide – the social context is real, felt, occasionally funny, as in the killing of the fly. The emphasis on this black mood prepares us for the black comedy to come when the suicide attempt goes wrong. There is also the sick joke that the tall man actually announces what he is going to do, but of course is not believed. The craving for sensation as an escape from reality is seen in the boy's thinking that the attempted hanging is better 'than seeing the Jungle Jim serial'. Sillitoe establishes a telling contrast between the black moods of the narrator and his family and the apparent calmness of the suicide. The boy's consciousness is revealed too, with his running thoughts about how his father would never hang himself and the idea of swapping stories with his mate – the hanging one for the Jungle Jim serial. With the grotesque failure there is an accompanying imagery from the boy's experience – 'his arms chafing like he was a scarecrow', 'as if he'd just took a dose of salts', and 'the bulb began circling round and round as though it was a space ship'. Such is the excitement generated that the boy feels frustrated at the failure – and perhaps sympathetic deep down that the man is frustrated too. With the arrival of the policeman there comes the 'rights and wrongs' debate, done in natural dialogue, with the law seen as the opponent of free will. The question is best summed up in the man's words: 'It is a fine thing if a bloke can't tek his own life.' But in the end he does the fine thing, leaving the boy sure in his own mind that he would never commit suicide no matter how bad he felt. The story has a twist but an effective and certainly probable one at the end, and is a salutary lesson to the narrator.

Uncle Ernest

This is unlike any of the other stories in that there is much more narrative and commentary and the dialogue lacks the locality of dialect. Its theme is the pathos of loneliness, the innocent way in which Ernest tries to combat it, and the way he is judged by others. It is a touching, moving story. When he meets the girls we sense his own longing for communication and companion-ship, and although they take advantage of him there is every reason for the reader to feel that this doesn't matter.

The early emphasis on the 'craftsmanship' of his eating shows how great Ernest's deprivation is. He is giving to food what he should be giving to life, and the guilt over the war experiences helps to explain him to us. Even when he first meets the girls he is thinking about the job he has to do that afternoon. As he listens to their quarrel over the cake, the anguish of his loneliness comes upon him – he has no one with whom he can communicate. After buying them the cakes he learns about their lives and feels that he is part of life again. They become, through their meetings, his family; but note how Alma takes advantage when she sees how dependent on them he is. In the words of the story, the girls were 'the only people he had to love'. The arrival of the police, the innuendo that is a threat, scares him, and ensures that his days of innocent loving and giving are over. He is forced to retreat from this new-found 'life' and return to the pub which will take away his past and obliterate the lonely futility of his present. As with 'On Saturday Afternoon' we are made aware of the obtrusive nature of the law, the med-dlesomeness of people, the poignancy of lonely and frustrated lives.

The Fishing-Boat Picture

First-person narrative again, this time from a postman looking back. The tone is relaxed, informal, and the short first section is concerned with the marriage-trap, followed by a laid-back account of the marriage itself. The narrator's cynical view that marriage is a kind of hire-purchase agreement is a clue to his personality, but we see that he is withdrawn whereas his wife wants him to be demonstrative. The phrase 'You're allus tired' speaks volumes about their incompatibility. The story is told from the perspective of the man who simply wants a quiet life. Consequently he mentions his wife's frustration at not having children in a tense way. When she runs off we sense a hint of regret, but the overwhelming impression is one of apathy.

There is quiet comedy in Kathy's return. Neither of them can voice their feelings, he because it is doubtful whether he has any positive ones, she because she is once more in that claustrophobic atmosphere which drove her out before. The contrast between them is admirably established, the common-place conversation about the coming war eventually leading to her wistful remark about Harry (the narrator) being 'never very excitable'. It is an understatement when we come to consider Harry's apathetic acceptance of everything that happens. Even while they are talking, when Harry asks the question about the house-painter, part of his mind is on the fact that he is missing the news on the wireless. And when she has gone – with the picture that is associated with their life together – Harry tells us 'it didn't take me long to get back to my book'.

His recovery of the picture from the pawnbroker's ('from the wreckage of other lives') and the knowledge that Kathy sold it, probably for the price of three pints of beer, leads to an expression of the strongest feeling of which Harry is capable. With Kathy's next visit the tension derives from her seeing the picture; she does not mention it, though she looks at it. With the continual 'borrowing' of money we realize (since Harry constantly tells us) that Kathy's one escape from her failed marriage is drink; she continually 'borrows' money to finance this. The symbol of the picture is always there, a record of their failure. Eventually she takes the picture again, but is killed (obviously she has been drinking) holding it. The final twist of the story comes with the knowledge that for the last six years

Kathy has been living with another man.

The inward suffering of Harry afterwards adds another dimension to the story. The key phrase is italicized – 'neither of us *did anything about it*'. This theme that it is too late is linked to the idea of non-communication of feelings, of being trapped in habit, of living for self. A wry, ironic humour plays over the whole story.

The Decline and Fall of Frankie Buller

The theme of the opening page is that we can't change anything: we have to accept what we become, though we can look back to what we were before. A stray experience can take us back into the past, and the first-person narrator goes back to a childhood which was at least in part influenced by the militaristic dreams and fantasies of a man who is still a youth, retarded and fixed in an earlier state without development. He is described by the narrator as a 'backward youth'. Frankie has been influenced by his father's account of the Great War and the fantasies he himself has conjured from it. The big lad – which is what he is – tells tall stories, his father's exploits existing for him as fact rather than fiction. The attack on the Sodom gang is full of graphic excitement: but the spectacle of boys playing at war has its wider echo in men about to embark on the horrific reality of war again. Part of the story's effect is the cut and thrust of dialect, but there is also Frankie's lonely place which is later destroyed by the lorry loads of rubble. As war nears, the pathos deepens with Frankie's final expedition which ends with disaster for him and is followed by the evacuation of the children. It is clear that he later lives in a world of make-believe, and the passage of time marks the permanence of his state, the Home Guard badge being the ultimate of his achievement (perhaps non-achievement would be more correct). We are aware too of the changes in the narrator – he revels in indulging his home accent as we feel that Sillitoe himself does in print – but the humanistic appraisal of Frankie's 'treatment' is full and uninhibited. The goodbye is unbearable. The moment of recognition is a direct one: books, which represent culture and some kind of intellectual attainment, cannot replace the essence of life in all its primitive simplicity.

Questions on *A Sillitoe Selection*

1 By a close examination of any *two* of the stories, show what effects Sillitoe achieves by the use of the first-person narrator.

2 Write about sadness or humour in any *three* of the stories.

3 Write about any characters in the stories whom you find sympathetic or unsympathetic, and say why you feel as you do about them.

4 Which incident in any three of the stories do you find the most exciting, and why?

5 In what ways does Sillitoe make use of the unexpected? You should refer to two or three stories in your answer.

6 Which story do you prefer and why? State your reasons clearly and quote in support of them.

7 Show how Sillitoe creates atmosphere in any two or three of the stories.

8 Show how Sillitoe understands either (a) various aspects of childhood or (b) the unusual character in any two or three of the stories.

Further reading

Other works by Alan Sillitoe

Novels

Key to the Door (Grafton Books 1986)

The Open Door (Grafton Books 1989): both of these feature the life of Arthur Seaton's brother, Brian.

The Death of William Posters (Grafton Books 1986)

A Tree on Fire (Grafton Books 1986)

The Flame of Life (Grafton Books 1986): a trilogy which travels from the Lincolnshire uplands to Algeria and back to London, and which deals with the dilemmas facing idealists in a corrupt society.

The Widower's Son (Grafton Books 1986): the story of a regular soldier who finds that army life has spoiled him for marriage.

Short stories and essays

Guzman, Go Home (Grafton Books 1986): especially 'The Rope Trick' which was originally intended as a novel sequel to *Loneliness*.

The Far Side of the Street (W. H. Allen 1988): a collection of stories chosen by Sillitoe himself.

Mountains and Caverns (W. H. Allen 1975): especially the autobiographical *The Long Piece*.

Collection

A Sillitoe Selection (Longman: Imprint Books, 1968): short stories, extracts from novels, autobiographical writing and critical commentary.

Other works of interest

Pre-1958 lower-middle-class novels

Hurry on Down (Penguin 1971) by John Wain: university drop-out rejects middle-class origins.

Lucky Jim (Penguin 1970) by Kingsley Amis: a lower-middle-class lecturer with anti-establishment attitudes.

That Uncertain Feeling (Penguin 1985) by Kingsley Amis: a provincial

Welsh librarian, his ambitions and marital problems.

Room at the Top (Penguin 1969) by John Braine: self-educated ruthless opportunist works in Town Hall in small Yorkshire town.

Post-1958

Billy Liar (Longman Paperback 1990) by Keith Waterhouse: a regional comedy about a youth who attempts to escape his dull family life through fantasy.

A Kind of Loving (Corgi: Black Swan 1986) by Stan Barstow: office-worker trapped into marriage.

This Sporting Life (Penguin 1986) by David Storey: Rugby League player becomes emotionally involved with his landlady.

A Kestrel for a Knave (Penguin 1969) by Barry Hines: a working-class fifteen-year-old finds pleasure in life only when flying his falcon.